NO AMOUNT OF HATE CAN QUENCH THE LOVE OF JESUS

# THE MARTYR'S OATH

*Living for the Jesus*
*They're Willing to Die For*

## JOHNNIE MOORE

*The nonfiction imprint of*
*Tyndale House Publishers, Inc.*

*The Lᴏʀᴅ is for me, so I will have no fear.*

*What can mere people do to me?*

PSALM 118:6, NLT

# CONTENTS

# INTRODUCTION

**I'LL NEVER FORGET** witnessing two thousand followers of Jesus take a martyr's oath.

I was in India attending the graduation at a Bible school founded by one of my mentors, the late Bishop M. A. Thomas. He not only knew firsthand the sting of persecution and the reality of holding a minority faith in a dangerous world, but he also knew the power of God's love to soften even the hardest heart. Born into poverty, he had walked across India to the area where God called him, wearing a giant placard with the gospel written on it so he could minister along the way. Once he arrived, he was thrown in prison, but he led so many inmates to Christ that the jailers kicked them all out. Those inmates became the first members of his church.

The ministry he founded in Kota in 1960 grew and eventually established ninety-five Bible institutes, sixty-one orphanages, forty-three thousand church plants, a hospital, medical clinics, substance abuse programs, and a publishing arm that prints literature in the countless languages of India.[1] And as a bishop, he oversaw ten thousand churches, many of which were planted in leper colonies. He survived at least fifteen assassination

x  ||  THE MARTYR'S OATH

attempts and walked with a limp because he was beaten so many times. Yet he wore a prominent cross around his neck to ensure extremists would recognize him. He was not ashamed of the cross.

Bishop Thomas made it clear that each of his students would be qualified for graduation only once they stood and confessed their willingness to serve Jesus even if it meant their death. They were to repeat after him, word for word, a martyr's oath. And they did—standing in an open-air tent next to a church that was too small to house them all. To this day, that church has a memorial next to its platform listing the names of the graduates who have already been martyred for Jesus.

One year extremists threw Molotov cocktails over the wall during a gathering the day before the graduation service, threatening to kill Bishop Thomas and burn the church. I can still hear Bishop Thomas's resonant voice booming over the microphone. "Listen to me!" he said. "Tomorrow there will be a service at this church. It will be a funeral service or a graduation service, but there will be a service!"

He was fearless.

The first time I witnessed the graduation, it shook my faith in a way I had never felt before. The temperatures soared over one hundred degrees without even a whiff of breeze, and an aroma of spices and humanity filled the still air as two thousand students pressed together with their family and friends. Unlike the American culture I was accustomed to, no one complained about the heat, the smell, or the inconvenience while singing "I Surrender All."

Word by word, the resolute roar of the students' voices rose from that dusty tent as they pledged their lives and deaths to

Jesus. I remember thinking that I was standing in the book of Acts, witnessing a raw, first-century Christianity that I'd been shielded from in the United States. I felt deprived yet suddenly spiritually alive in an entirely new way.

My faith finally made sense. All the disparate parts of the New Testament came together in my heart as I witnessed this authentic expression of faith in Jesus. *Real* faith in Jesus. These bold brothers and sisters weren't just willing to live for Jesus; they were willing to die for him.

I asked myself—as I have a thousand times since—*Why are so few of us in America willing to live for Jesus when others are so willing to die for him?* Seeing Jesus through the eyes of the persecuted church transformed me.

I've written this book because I believe seeing your faith through their eyes will change you, too. My prayer for you is that their stories will change your life in a way you desperately need. Perhaps it will change you in a way you don't even know you need.

I've also written this book because the Bible declares, "If one part [of the body] suffers, all the parts suffer with it" (1 Corinthians 12:26, NLT). I feel like we barely care or barely know the stories of our persecuted brothers and sisters. Either is an unspeakable tragedy. As my friends at Open Doors International are fond of saying, "If you follow Jesus, there's a part of your family you need to know: those who are suffering and those who will die for Jesus."

Some estimate that every five minutes, a Christian is martyred for the faith.[2] For many, avoiding martyrdom is as simple as writing or even saying that they renounce their faith in Jesus. For these martyred believers, the gospel is so precious, the comfort of the Holy Spirit so tangible, and the example of those

Christians who have come before them so compelling that they will not weaken or renounce their faith—regardless of the cost.

It has cost them their lives. The gospel has cost most of us nothing.

My team and I have crisscrossed the world, recorders in hand, to gather reports from survivors, asking them to tell us what God is doing in and through ordinary people who meet extraordinary circumstances with overcoming faith.

In these pages, I relate what they said, using their exact words. We've transcribed their stories, connecting each with observations about the suffering they face and the lessons to be learned. In every story, as in the declarations of those graduates from Bishop Thomas's school, you will find a willingness to live and to die for Christ.

Like the family we met in the Middle East who found faith in Christ as refugees fleeing the Syrian war. They were jihadists themselves until they encountered Jesus in a miraculous way. The news made it all the way back to one of their adult siblings in Syria, prompting a strongly worded message in reply, guaranteeing their death by crucifixion if they did not return to Islam. The new follower of Jesus replied to his brother-in-law, "We are willing to die for Jesus, but please do not crucify us. We are not worthy of dying in the same way as our Savior."

Unlike the jihadist martyrs gaining the attention—and fear—of the world, these followers of Jesus are not seeking to die in order to *earn* a place in heaven. They are willing to die as an expression of gratitude for *having already received* the gift of God's salvation through Jesus and his promise to live together in a real, eternal heaven. They die with prayers of love and forgiveness on their lips. In their dying breaths, they profess Jesus' kindness and love for the world.

And that's another reason I've written this book. In a time when we are witnessing martyrdom and persecution akin to that endured by our brothers and sisters in the first century, we are also seeing the same miraculous works as those days in the early church. Nearly every day, a terrorist is encountering Jesus on a road to Damascus. There are countless "apostle Pauls" emerging in our time. Many of them are converted as miraculously as he was, and many of them will suffer and die as he did. All of them believe that Jesus is the only real hope in the world.

First-century persecution in the twenty-first century—while horrific and evil—is also producing a first-century harvest of millions coming to follow Jesus in the most miraculous ways and from the most unlikely places.

Here are their true stories, and my hope is that by the end of this book, you, too, will be willing to take the Martyr's Oath, which I have included at both the beginning and the end of this book. The title of each chapter is taken from the oath, and the stories within each chapter illustrate what it means to live out this statement.

If you are ready to stand with Christians around the world in harm's way and take the Martyr's Oath, then go to www.MartyrsOath.com and take your stand.

More important, I hope you learn how to live for the Jesus they are willing to die for, wherever you are and whether it costs you anything—or everything.

*Johnnie Moore*
*The Netherlands*
*2016*

# THE MARTYR'S OATH

**I AM A FOLLOWER OF JESUS.** I believe he lived and walked among us, was crucified for our sins, and was raised from the dead, according to the Scriptures. I believe he is the King of the earth, who will come back for his church.

As he has given his life for me, so I am willing to give my life for him. I will use every breath I possess to boldly proclaim his gospel. Whether in abundance or need, in safety or peril, in peace or distress, I will not—I cannot—keep quiet. His unfailing love is better than life, and his grace compels me to speak his name even if his name costs me everything. Even in the face of death, I will not deny him. And should shadow and darkness encroach upon me, I will not fear, for I know he is always with me.

Though persecution may come, I know my battle is not against flesh but against the forces of evil. I will not hate those whom God has called me to love. Therefore, I will forgive when ridiculed, show mercy when struck, and love when hated. I will clothe myself with meekness and kindness so those around me may see the face of Jesus reflected in me, especially if they abuse me.

I have taken up my cross; I have laid everything else down. I know my faith could cost me my life, but I will follow and love Jesus until the end, whenever and however that end may come. Should I die for Jesus, I confess that my death is not to achieve salvation but in gratitude for the grace I've already received. I will not die to earn my reward in heaven, but because Jesus has already given me the ultimate reward in the forgiveness of my sins and the salvation of my soul.

For me to live is Christ; for me to die is gain.

*In Jesus' name,*

*Amen.*

# CHAPTER 1

# I AM A FOLLOWER OF JESUS

*We are hard-pressed on every side, yet not crushed;*
*we are perplexed, but not in despair; persecuted, but*
*not forsaken; struck down, but not destroyed.*

2 CORINTHIANS 4:8-9, NKJV

**MORE CHRISTIANS WERE MARTYRED** for their faith in the twentieth century than in all previous centuries combined.[1]

Some people are fond of saying that the persecution Christians are now facing is just history repeating itself. They suggest it's the same as it has ever been, but that is not the case. Persecution against Christians has dramatically escalated, and the scale of the brutality has worsened.

Open Doors International, an organization that ranks levels of persecution around the world, has noted that, conservatively, more than 7,100 Christians were killed for their faith in 2015. That's nearly double the number killed in 2014 and more than triple the number killed in 2013.[2] The actual number is probably much higher. Statistics are hard to come by in countries that behead, burn alive, and enslave people.

It's as if Satan himself is playing for keeps, employing astonishing efforts to wipe the followers of Jesus from the face of the earth—to finish us off and to do it with all the spectacle he possibly can. Yet Christianity is now the largest religion in the world, with more than two billion believers worldwide.[3]

What is it about Christianity that has caused so much hate to be unleashed against it?

It comes down to what we believe, which I've summarized in the Martyr's Oath:

I am a follower of Jesus. I believe he lived and walked among us, was crucified for our sins, and was raised from the dead, according to the Scriptures. I believe he is the King of the earth, who will come back for his church.

In his day, the apostle Paul wrote that "the message of the cross is foolishness to those who are perishing" (1 Corinthians 1:18). And we see that same opinion shared today, especially as Christian faith is pushed out of the public arena in secular states. But in some parts of the world, believing in Christ is seen as worse than foolishness. It's viewed as a threat, and it comes with a death sentence.

Under Communist regimes, where the state demands full and unquestioning loyalty, Christians' beliefs that Jesus is Lord and that our citizenship is in heaven are viewed as seditious. And in the Islamic world, believing that Jesus is the only way to God the Father is viewed as blasphemy.

As we consider at the outset of the book what it means to be followers of Jesus, I want you to read these stories from Christians in Nigeria, in their own words. In Nigeria, simply following Jesus has cost some faithful believers nearly everything.

## DORIS, UCHE, AND GABRIEL ‖ *Nigeria*

*Christmas Eve 2010 in Jos, Nigeria: the streets are buzzing with last-minute shoppers in a crowded suburb. Doris, a widow of just one year, browses the shops. The mother of five needs just one more item to start her cooking.*

*Middle-aged Uche, sporting short-cropped hair and a mustache, is walking from work to the market to buy supplies for his family's Christmas celebration.*

*Gabriel is a father of two, with a slender build and wearing a thin, short-sleeved white oxford shirt with no pocket. He tends his mother's fabric shop and notices something is off. He has come to this part of town just to help her after taking time off from his own work. While busying himself, he sees a few men drop off a package at the shop. He thinks it's strange, but like other shop owners and shoppers, he doesn't do anything about it—it's Christmas Eve, and everyone just wants to get home to their families.*

*As the clock ticks toward 7:00 p.m., a series of blasts shakes the market. A transit bus bursts into flames, streaking the night sky with orange and red. Burning shops, homes, and automobiles add an eerie, dancing light. Building walls are sprayed with black film. The smell of chemicals, heat, and charred wood permeates the air. The streets are littered with food, clothes, and body parts.*

*Doris, Uche, and Gabriel are just a few of the hundreds who have faced constant hardships since the blasts. Yet they are lucky.*

*Nearby, two churches were attacked, and another bombing targeted a Christian area. In all, more than eighty funerals were held in the few days following the attack.*

*Yet the church remains, and the survivors choose to remain. They continue to speak Jesus' name and to tell of his grace with boldness. Silence would mean security. Fleeing would mean safety. But it isn't about security and safety to them. It's about the privilege to be the light of Jesus in the very darkest places.*

 **DORIS**

"I was in the market, and I was on my way back when a bomb went off near a bridge. I had stopped to buy spices so I could cook. The bomb went off, and I was lifted off the ground. When I fell down, I tried to stand up. But I fell down again, and I realized my leg had been blown off.

After the accident, I was taken to the hospital, and my leg had to be amputated. Now I walk slowly. I fall down. I don't even know who paid for my medical bills. It might have been the government, but I don't know for sure.

My church has been helpful. I have five children, and they support me as well. I live with my daughter and her husband. I am following the Lord strongly because he spared me. Many died that day, so I have a lot that I owe him. I always thank him. Since he spared me, it means he wants me to carry on his work."

## UCHE

“ God has blessed me with three children. I am a metalworker, and on Christmas Eve, I got off work early for the celebration. I went to the market very close to where I live to buy things for our Christmas celebration. I heard the sound of a bomb nearby, and when it went off, I lost both of my legs.

They took me to the hospital, and from there I spent months in the hospital. My colleagues helped pay my medical bills. I finished the treatments and then went back home with two artificial legs. I still have expensive medicines I have to buy. My wife would not stay. She left me and the children.

I can't go back to my job, so it is hard to pay school fees for my children. We struggle to pay for where we live, but we cannot afford to move. Life isn't easy for our family.

From the beginning, I gave my life to God. I know he will never leave me. Whatever the reason for why this happened to me, I know he will meet my needs. ”

## GABRIEL

“ I am a worker and have two children. My mom has her own fabric shop in a market.

On Christmas Eve, I took off work to help her at her shop because she had lots of customers coming. I noticed Muslims came and left something nearby. But I didn't pay attention, because I was busy. Around 7:00 p.m., the bomb blew up in the shop.

It killed many people. That's how I got this injury on my leg. I was rushed to a nearby hospital, where they started treatment. There were not enough doctors to treat me. I had my leg amputated and now have an artificial limb.

Now, I've been buying medicine day in and day out. I cannot work at my old job. My mother is aging. Her business has collapsed. She is depressed. I can't work enough, and I can't care for her. My children are still small. They look up to me. But I cannot even pick them up because I can't lift heavy things now. My injuries handicap me.

My mother depends on me. She needs me to help care for her financially. But I depend on others to give me simple jobs. I have to care for my wife and children, too, so I need consistent work.

I'm telling you, this is real life for us. It's only through the help of God that we have survived.

We all believe in Christ. He is our personal Lord and Savior, and with him all things are possible. He is our source. Man cannot give you these things, so I stand strongly in my faith. Without him we can do nothing. 〞

**HANNAH** || *Nigeria*

*Sixteen-year-old Abigail was asleep in her school's dormitory during finals week. Only one assignment stood between her and the close of the school year. She would soon be home and enjoying the life of a teenage girl.*

As she slept, Abigail didn't know of the phone calls coming to her area from neighboring villages, warning that the terrorist group Boko Haram was on the way. She didn't know of the failed attempts to get more security to her school. She probably didn't even know that Boko Haram had threatened to burn schools and kidnap children. All she knew was that she was surrounded by her friends and classmates, her parents lived nearby, security forces were outside her dorm, and she had just one more assignment to finish.

Today, Abigail has been featured in a Boko Haram video released to prove that the 276 schoolgirls kidnapped on the night of April 14, 2014, are still alive. Obviously under duress, she states in her native Hausa language, "Our parents should take heart. Talk to the government so that we can be allowed to go home. Please come to our rescue. The aircraft have come and killed many of us. We are really suffering here. There is no food to eat, no good water to drink."

A terrorist then takes to the screen to repeat their same demands, that the government release imprisoned Boko Haram fighters. "Or we will never release these girls."

Reports of the kidnapped girls electrified the media within thirty-six hours of the assault on their school. The kidnapping arrested the attention of the entire world, with millions tweeting #BringBackOurGirls. Even former US First Lady Michelle Obama joined in the social-media advocacy. Yet all civilian and government efforts couldn't convince Boko Haram of the evil they'd done. They kept the girls, forcibly converted them to Islam, and made some of them sexual slaves and others soldiers.

Today, a "BBOG" Facebook page features scores of likes.[4] An *outspoken BBOG activist group helped elect a new Nigerian president whose campaign promises included finding the girls. With that hope dashed, the BBOG campaign continues staging protests and rallies to keep the vanished girls before the eyes of the world.*

*Hannah, Abigail's mother, has been in the news herself, criticizing the government for not rescuing the girls and blaming it on the fact that her village is poor.*

*Around 135 of the original girls have now escaped or been released. But not Abigail. She's still lost.*

*Hannah wears a head wrapper made of a bright geometric print that matches her dress. She holds her head upright and speaks in declarative statements tinged with defiance. She talks freely until she comes to the end of her story. Then she speaks wistfully, with long pauses. And then she weeps. She just weeps. She is grateful to God for the four children she has, yet nothing takes the place of her baby.*

*She is spirited. She is passionate. She is a mother. She is determined. She is hopeful. She is angry.[5]*

"It was an awful night, April 14, 2014. We had no information, no idea, no news, nothing. We just heard gunshots coming from the direction of her boarding school. *Lord, my daughter!* All my knowledge, my brain, my head, my strength, my energy went out to that school.

We had heard they planned to attack schools and kidnap kids. I called my sister. She didn't know anything. She said, "Just give up for the night." But I said, "I [am] going to the school for my baby!"

My husband stopped me. He said, "There is security in

the school." But I could hear the gunshots, so I planned to go fight. I grabbed some rocks because we have rocks everywhere.

It was the long, long night.

There were normally fourteen or fifteen security soldiers. But they could not win. We don't know what happened. But we heard Boko Haram from 11:00 p.m. until 4:00 in the morning—shooting, burning. At 4:00 a.m. it became quiet, so we rushed to the school. The girls were gone. We saw their uniforms, their dresses, everything scattered everywhere. We thought the girls had tried to escape or the security had rescued them or something of that nature. But the whole school was burned. They destroyed the roof. They burned out everything.

We met one girl, and I asked her, "Where are the girls?" She said, "I don't know." I kept crying, "Where is my baby?" I called her name, "Abigail!" The girl said, "Maybe she went home." She didn't know what happened. I screamed, "She is not at home!" Then I asked her more questions. The girl said that night she was not feeling well. She was sleeping in some other dormitory when the noise from Boko Haram woke her up as they burned the building. Before she came out, she realized the heat of the fire was too much, so she climbed out the window and onto a tree. She climbed down, then climbed over a fence and ran away. That's how she escaped.

We talked to her and then stayed at the school, hoping to see our girls. After an hour or two, some girls came walking toward the school. We rushed to them and said,

"What's happened?" They said, "Boko Haram has kidnapped and packed up all of them."

"How did they pack them up?" I asked. They said, "In a truck." The escaped girls said they packed them in trucks and cars and carted them away.

It was a government-run "comprehensive boarding school," so the boys went in the morning for the lectures. In the evening, after closing hours, the boys would go home. But the girls stayed in the dormitory. So the boys were secured because they were home with their parents. But the girls . . . the girls . . . that happened to them!

I talked to many girls. Many girls. I tried to sort out where my baby was. I have a cousin who was with her, who escaped. She said Abigail was in the truck close to the driver. Abigail couldn't jump out. My cousin called to her that she was dropping out of the truck, but Abigail just couldn't make it. She couldn't escape.

Another girl, before she escaped the next day, said she saw my baby sleeping. Abigail was tired because as they were driving, their truck broke down. So they had to trek on foot to the Sambisa Forest. That's where they are to this day.

Now there is a negotiator with Boko Haram, and they got fifteen of the girls and interviewed them on December 25 last year. They still have hundreds of girls in captivity. The military is combing the forest, still looking for them. They say the place is too dangerous. They can't enter with firepower because that could harm the girls. Maybe Boko Haram will harm the girls. Maybe Boko Haram will use the girls as a human shield.

My baby was not yet sixteen, but now she is eighteen.
She was writing her final paper. I don't know where she
might be. I am hoping that one day we will see them.
Prayer is the only key to success. With God, it is possible.
He is a great God. My baby . . .

Make no mistake. Both the Jos market bombing and Boko Haram's
kidnapping of schoolgirls targeted the victims because of their
Christianity. The extremists have gone from one Christian village
to the next, terrorizing Nigeria's Christians. In one province alone,
more than 70 percent of the churches have been destroyed.

Jesus tells his disciples, "If you do not carry your own cross and
follow me, you cannot be my disciple. But don't begin until you
count the cost" (Luke 14:27-28, NLT). For many Christians around the
world, and for those who tell their stories here, they have counted
the cost. Whatever they suffer, whether they give up their health,
their livelihoods, or even their lives, they recognize that Jesus is
greater than it all.

I wonder how many of us in the United States have counted the
cost of following Jesus—I mean *really* counted the cost. For some
of us, we may think we have. We just don't think we need Jesus
very much. Jesus is the ultimate "value add" to whatever version of
the good life we've fashioned, the capstone to a life well lived. He
gives unilateral approval to our decisions and may get us out of a
jam now and then, but he doesn't require much from us. We don't
demand much of him, so he can't demand much of us.

I want to draw your attention to Gabriel's brave words: "We

all believe in Christ. He is our personal Lord and Savior, and with him all things are possible. He is our source. Man cannot give you these things, so I stand strongly in my faith. Without him we can do nothing."

*Without him we can do nothing.*

In our self-reliant, individualistic culture, these words are radical. They are an acknowledgment of Jesus' lordship, his authority over every area of our lives. And Jesus' authority is one that we willingly, lovingly, and eagerly must submit to.

What does it mean for those of us who are in the most prosperous nation on earth to join with those who are losing their lives for believing in Jesus? What does counting the cost look like for us?

These brave believers who are so confident and fearless in their testimony, even in the face of horrific loss, show us the way. For sure, believers around the world need our prayers, and they need our financial support. It's not unusual for social support systems to be nonexistent for Christians in countries where Christian persecution is common. And those Christians who manage to escape are often not allowed to work in the countries that have granted them refuge, leaving them in jeopardy. They need *our* help.[6]

But we also need *their* help.

For all that we may be doing to help them, they also help us. They inspire us to a deeper place in our commitment to Jesus. They inspire us to *live* for the Jesus they are willing to *die* for. Their testimonies call us to take our own faith more seriously, and they lead us to discover the true power of Jesus.

# CHAPTER 2

# I AM WILLING TO GIVE MY LIFE

*Hold firmly to the word of life; then, on the day of Christ's*
*return, I will be proud that I did not run the race in vain and*
*that my work was not useless. But I will rejoice even if I lose*
*my life, pouring it out like a liquid offering to God.*

PHILIPPIANS 2:16-17, NLT

**BOKO HARAM,** the terrorist group responsible for kidnapping two hundred schoolgirls from the Government Girls Secondary School in Chibok, Nigeria, is the deadliest foe of Christianity in the world right now—far more lethal to Christianity than ISIS, to whom Boko Haram has pledged allegiance. Human rights advocates note that Boko Haram killed 6,644 people in 2014—more even than ISIS did. The actual figures are probably even greater. Boko Haram has always outpaced ISIS in both scale and brutality.

When it comes to Christianity, a Boko Haram leader has been totally transparent about the group's intentions. He says they are "booby-trapping and blowing up every church that we are able to reach, and killing all those we find from the citizens of the cross."[1]

There is one settled fact about Boko Haram: they aim to ethnically cleanse Christians from Nigeria before doing the same across all of Africa. If they could, Boko Haram would wipe all Christians off the face of the planet unless we were willing to convert to their extremist form of Islam.

Northern Nigeria has therefore become the front line in the battle between Christianity and extremist Islam in Africa. Even in 2012—before ISIS—"more Christians were killed in Northern Nigeria . . . than in the rest of the world combined."[2]

It is here that we meet an extraordinary young woman named Rose, whose courage in the face of unthinkable persecution exemplifies the sacrificial spirit that is the very heartbeat of the Martyr's Oath.

 **ROSE** ‖ *Nigeria*

*Rose's skin glows and a timid smile plays across her face. As she speaks, she studies the long, gold drapery in the coffee shop and glances through the glass tabletop at the floor. She rests one hand in another, favoring one arm. Nigerian pedestrians on a crowded sidewalk outside make loud, declarative statements that serve as both questions and answers. Over the din, it's difficult to hear Rose's rasp, which rises barely above a whisper. Her tone isn't natural. It's clearly the product of some awful story, some terrible memory.*

*Otherwise, the young woman looks every bit a soccer mom from Africa. Black hair pulled straight back, kind eyes, a pleasant expression. It seems as if she would be discussing kids and her husband with a friend. But if she turns, you see the labyrinth of scars on the back of her neck and you notice the favored arm is mangled. When she speaks, she doesn't tell about a Saturday soccer game or a husband's laughable attempt at coaching. Instead, with calm composure, she tells of how she once lived in northeast Nigeria under threat of Boko Haram—and of the night her husband was beheaded before her eyes, followed by two of her children.*

*Saying two simple words was all that separated Rose from life and death—Allahu Akbar. But her faith refused to let her say them. Instead, she offered a one-word prayer: "Jesus." She was willing to give her life for Jesus. After all, he had given his life for her.*

I was running and running. They had sliced my arm, so I took off my shirt and wrapped it around to stop the bleeding. But three people caught up and pushed me. I fell to the ground. They started slicing my neck. They said, "Say Allahu Akbar!"

I said, "No, I won't!"

With every rejection they sliced at my neck with their swords and chanting with greater determination, "Say it! Allahu Akbar, Allahu Akbar!" Instead I chanted, "Jesus! Jesus!" until I could no longer speak.

Even then, I kept trying to say his name, "Jesus!"

My husband and I had been home with two of our three children. He was a police officer. My oldest daughter was visiting another village. That's when my husband heard shots outside and said, "Those don't sound like police arms. It must be Boko Haram."

He said an official had given him permission to defend himself if they ever came. "These people are here to kill us," he said. "But before they kill us, I will put up a fight."

He tried.

When the terrorists busted in, my husband shot every one that came through the door. He had thirty-six rounds and fired them all. I saw eight people fall dead, and I watched others run away injured. Then he was out of bullets. They came in and ordered him to lie down. That's when they cut off my husband's head entirely, then our children's heads.

I crouched as though I was going to lie down, but then I took off running. I was six months pregnant and didn't feel well. They reached out with a sword and sliced my arm as I ran by. That didn't stop me. I ran, but they caught me and pushed me to the ground. They sliced my neck deeply. I was bleeding so much that they left me for dead.

The attack came on Wednesday night, and I lay where I fell until Friday. It rained. The wind blew. Mosquitoes were all over me. I had to swat them away. Then, health workers came to clear away corpses. I heard them. I lifted my hand. They said, "Someone is alive!"

That was the first miracle I ever experienced. How could I lie there for more than thirty-six hours? Bleeding as I was, yet I survived. It was God who protected me. God who allowed me to survive.

I spent three months in the intensive care unit. My family paid some of my medical bills and visited me. I ate food through a tube. They said the tube would be permanent. Then missionaries in the area recognized I needed better care and took me to a Christian hospital. The doctors did a few operations on me and also took out the feeding tube. The nerves in my arm are still badly damaged and painful. I lost the baby I was carrying. I lost my husband. I lost my sons.

When I finally got home, my in-laws had taken all of our possessions. They said I should marry my late husband's brother to get back our belongings, but I refused. They took custody of my sole surviving child, my twelve-year-old daughter. Later I was able to recover custody of her, and then we moved to live with my parents.

A few years later, at about ten o'clock one morning, Boko Haram started bombing and burning my parents' village. Can you believe it—a second attack? I found my daughter, my mom, and my sister, and we ran. We escaped to another town, just barely. We reached out again to the missionaries.

They set up a shop for me, but thieves robbed it. I grew a garden, farmed for a while, then some people taught me how to sew and I opened another shop. My father said, "Don't worry; life is more than possessions."

He was right. My daughter is behind in school by a couple of grades, but she's taking exams to catch up.

I am thankful to God for sparing my life. I'm grateful for people who have come along who are like a new family to me. We need prayers because of how those people are running around continuing to kill others. 🙶

✝

I read something about Americans that I think is true: the first rule in our culture is self-preservation. We do everything in our power to extend our lives, to protect our lives, to improve our lives, and to guard our lives, but this is not an idea we've inherited from Christianity. The prevailing characteristic I have found among persecuted believers is not self-preservation but self-sacrifice.

It's just very simple to them, and I think it ought to be simple to us. Our circumstances ought not to change the way we think about Jesus.

Jesus gave his life for them, and so they are willing to give their lives for him. It's not just about sacrificing their lives, either. Most of these brothers and sisters—because that's what they are; they are family—had to sacrifice a thousand other necessities and securities before they faced the final challenge. For many of us in the West, if we sacrifice at all, it is our luxuries, which isn't much of a sacrifice.

Those of us who are blessed with security and freedom have a tendency to rationalize our faith when we think through circumstances like Rose's.

This book isn't about easy things, and it doesn't contain easy stories. But for Rose's sake, let's just think about this together, not within the context of someone else's life, but within the context of our own lives.

"Why wouldn't you just say 'Allahu Akbar' if Jesus will forgive you anyway?" we might ask. "Then we could live to fight another day and maybe even witness to the love of Christ to those who came to convert us."

That we even think of such a "way out" of the situation might be a terrible warning about the condition of our own hearts. For, as Jesus says, "Whatever is in your heart determines what you say" (Matthew 12:34, NLT).

In my experience, calculations like these don't even enter the minds of believers in the world's most persecuted places. Instead they say, "It's not possible for me to deny Jesus." They're too committed for that. Their faith is an inseparable part of their identity. They have been made "new creations" (see 2 Corinthians 5:17).

We look at them strangely from within our safe Christianity, but these days I'm wondering whether it is even Christianity that we have within our safety. Do we have authentic faith, or do we have a "form of godliness with no power" (see 2 Timothy 3:5)? It's worth asking the question, because Jesus says, "Everyone who denies me here on earth, I will also deny before my Father in heaven" (Matthew 10:33, NLT).

We may see the simple, sacrificial faith of those who are persecuted as peculiar because we have become so accustomed to our religious maneuvering that we do not even realize how far we've drifted from the purity and simplicity of living for Jesus.

Could it be that we are simply using Jesus as a means to assuage our consciences as we live for ourselves? We self-medicate on religion so we don't feel quite so bad about our total self-centeredness, our unabashed obsession with ourselves, our things, our future, and our lives.

We look with such peculiarity at the willingness of our brothers and sisters to die, and they look at us in the same way. They are totally confused that our faith costs us almost nothing—maybe 10 percent of our income and the occasional remark at work. Do we really serve the same Jesus if we're content to allow our faith to cost us so little?

Here's the solution: long before our faith costs us our *life*, it has to cost us our *self*.

Selfishness, self-centeredness, and self-preservation in all its manicured forms will only lead us down a dangerous path. Our obsession with self is antithetical to the way of Jesus. As Dietrich Bonhoeffer said, "When Christ calls a man, he bids him come and die."[3]

Self-sacrifice seems to take from us the life we're looking for, but it is actually the secret to finding life. At least that's what Jesus taught us. He said, "Anyone who loves their life will lose it" (John 12:25). But often, while we say we believe Jesus, we don't actually believe, because we don't live in the way he has told us to live. He said, "All who love me will do what I say" (John 14:23, NLT).

Rose was willing to give everything for Jesus because he gave everything for her.

He also gave everything for *us*. The question is, are we willing to do the same for him?

# CHAPTER 3

# I WILL BOLDLY PROCLAIM HIS GOSPEL

*I am in chains now, still preaching this message as God's ambassador.*
*So pray that I will keep on speaking boldly for him, as I should.*

EPHESIANS 6:20, NLT

**THERE'S ONE WORD** that will get you in prison more quickly than any other: *evangelism*. Keeping your faith to yourself will sometimes allow you to fly under the radar in certain places, but trouble arrives the moment you start to live your faith in any kind of public form.

The problem with following Jesus is that you can't actually do it passively and invisibly. It seeps through your words and your actions. True Christianity cannot be hidden or contained. Eventually it will spill over. Christianity is not just a set of beliefs; it is a lifestyle. We live a life of love, and because of the transformation God has performed in us, we naturally tell others about him. If we aren't inclined to do so, then we aren't really experiencing the power of

God in our lives. As James writes, "Faith without deeds is dead" (James 2:26).

While no one should be forced to change their religion, everyone should have an opportunity to choose what they want to believe. In many countries, there are state laws forbidding evangelism and conversion. Laws around the world ought not to just protect religious expression. They ought to also grant each person the right to convert. Instead, living and sharing one's faith marks believers for special persecution at the hands of these governments, and it sometimes sets the stage for moments when God's power shows up in miraculous ways—as in Andrew's life.

**ANDREW** || *Middle East*

*The story Andrew tells can be summarized by answer D to this multiple-choice question:*

*In which country was Andrew imprisoned for his faith?*

*D: All of the above.*

*After coming to Christ in Communist Eritrea, Andrew was imprisoned for his faith. After that, he ministered in another country, where he was also imprisoned, and then in another, where he was imprisoned again. I'm not mentioning where this was because Andrew—also not his real name—is still very much at work (and at risk). Revealing his location or work could cost him his life. The truth is that he's okay* with that. What he's not okay with is stopping the explosive growth of the church in the areas where he's working. So we're protecting his identity in order to protect the churches that are growing because of his ministry.

Andrew is like a modern-day apostle Paul. Persecuted, deported, expatriated, imprisoned, falsely accused—Andrew has seen it all, experienced it all. Yet he suffers, forgives, and preaches on. He is buoyant and energetic. His approach to sharing Jesus is "to everyone, everywhere," so wherever he goes, he believes he was sent there as a witness for Jesus.

He realizes more than most people that life can be cut short at any time, so he speaks rapidly as he tells his stories of persecution, as if they are minor inconveniences. He races straight to the stories of the great salvations he has witnessed. From the judge who came to Christ before sentencing him, to the prisoners he met, to the first Muslim man he led to Christ in his new home—a man he later learned was a spy for Osama bin Laden.

    I grew up as a Communist in Eritrea. I was a firm believer in this philosophy. But when Communism fell in 1991 all across the globe, I questioned it. Finally I came to faith in Jesus and started serving him in ministry. From 1991 to 1998 was a golden time of serving the Lord and planting churches in Eritrea.

    Things changed in 1998 when the war with Ethiopia began. The government was fearful of losing control. They believed churches were spreading Western propaganda, and they wanted to keep spreading Communist ideology. They targeted young people with Communist propaganda.

They sent letters to churches telling them they had to close their doors. Officially, there was religious freedom, but the government started persecuting the church. The local police and courts all began to make their case against us with falsified information.

One day, officials came to me and said, "You must leave this village." I said, "It's my right to preach. What I'm doing is legal." The authorities gathered false accusers from the community to claim our church was a disturbance. In a few weeks, I was set to appear before the court. The church was praying like never before. We knew this was out of our hands. What could we do? The police, the municipalities, and the courts were all coming against us. We could only pray to God.

Before the hearing, I met with the judge privately. I said, "Look, we haven't done anything wrong." The judge said, "I know. Just last night, God revealed himself to me in my dreams and said, 'Don't touch this man.'" After the judge told of the miraculous appearance, he said, "Can you give me a Bible?" Before long, he came to Jesus. The church rejoiced! Also at that time many Muslims started coming to Jesus, just as they are now.

When the trial came, the false accusers began stating their case. One by one, the judge exposed the foolishness of their arguments. "They are praising and shouting," the accusers complained. The judge said, "Is that bad?" One by one the accusations came, but the newly converted judge put them to shame. The case was dismissed. Of course, at the time the judge kept his faith a secret to the community.

Eritrean law provided the opportunity for the church to counterclaim, since we had been wrongfully accused of breaking the law and disturbing the community. But we responded and said we had no desire to bring charges against anyone. It was our testimony to the community. But from then on, they were watching me.

Soon the authorities came to me and said, "We're at war, and you have to fight for your country now." So I spent two years training at a military camp, but I maintained my faith. I thought, *Now I will have a ministry at the military camp!* That's how I became the first evangelist in the military camps of Eritrea. From morning until night, I thought, *I have to serve the Lord here.*

In the Eritrean military, it was forbidden to have a Bible or any sort of Christian literature. They would burn it. But I was given favor from the Lord. My military leader was a born-again believer! Other Christians were amazed with what we could do there. We held baptisms right in the camp and developed a strong network of churches.

Then one day, authorities put me and forty others in prison in the camp. I said, *I have to serve the Lord, even in prison.* They soon released all of us and said we needed to finish our military training.

Yet once our training was finally complete, six church leaders were sent to prison once again. The authorities found spiritual books in English and Arabic that we distributed to people in the military. I heard a military official say, "Unless we kill these people, they will not stop!"

They decided they would kill us in front of everyone,

to scare the young people, to make them fear the government. For two years, we waited on death row. We continued to get Christian literature smuggled to us, and we would hide it. We were never killed.

The conditions are rough and inhumane. You would only eat once a day. You are given access to a toilet only every three to four days. Most of the rooms are about four feet by four feet. As many as forty to fifty people are crammed into small units. Often the prisoners sleep on top of each other, bodies overlapping. I could sometimes not resist stretching my legs. Others were the same. Then there would be feet in your face, in your stomach.

They would push in more and more prisoners. I would put my nose up to a small crack in the wall to breathe in fresh air. Now I give thanks to God all the time for fresh air and clean water.

"Will you leave Christ?" they would ask. And they would stomp on our feet. They would take us out into the hot sun at noon and leave us there for hours. They would lay us down on our stomachs in the sand and bind our hands to our feet in the "helicopter" method.[1] And while we baked there in the hot sun, they would often come hit our feet, sometimes drawing blood. Sometimes people even died.

But the Lord provided a way out for me. As the war with Ethiopia dragged on, the war zone began to creep closer and closer to this camp, because it was near the border. Before long, bombings happened right near our prison. The military officials and guards scattered, leaving me and my friends to go free. God saved my life through this war.

A few years later, I thought, *I know I'm going to die, so I might as well serve the Lord!* All of my experiences helped me understand how my life could end in an instant. So I moved to a new nation to start a ministry to Arabs.

Three friends and I began a new ministry, with much success. We decided to preach to the Muslims. We witnessed to our neighbors and on the streets all throughout the city. It was dangerous, but sometimes we would pass out Christian literature at the bus station. We'd go for five minutes or so and then hurry out.

One day we decided to go to a hospital to pray for patients. We didn't realize it, but we walked into a hospital for women. It's not allowed for men, but somehow we were able to walk right in. Once we were in, we prayed for the expectant mothers there. We prayed for them and shared Jesus with them as well. We left. But soon we were chased down by the hospital security. They told us that we should never have been allowed inside. We were sent to prison over that issue. They held us on charges of theft. I had about $200 US in my pocket that my brother had sent me, so the police took it.

The prison was like a new mission field for us. We met one believer who told us to be strong, and we were so encouraged. Once again, we decided, we would preach Jesus. *Why not bring glory to God?* I thought. We told the inmates about Jesus. Prison officials became angry, and some of them would slap us across the face. We became known as "the people that pray in Jesus' name." Compared to Eritrea, this prison was nowhere near as bad.

We went before a court that was ruled by Sharia law.
But we had a lawyer who argued that in our country it was
okay to pray in the hospital. The court said that it wasn't
but ruled that we wouldn't be subject to imprisonment.
Instead, we would have to pay a fine.

I decided to study Arabic to minister to Muslims in the
Arab world. I had to leave my two friends to pursue this
new dream. I went to another country and studied for two
years. There I found a Muslim man who allowed me to witness to him for a while.

The man told me that he wasn't sleeping at night. I
gave some Scriptures to him, and soon he could sleep.
Then I gave him a Bible. The man told me of an earlier time
when he woke up and his light was on. But he had turned
it off. He turned it off again and then fell back asleep.
When he awoke again, once again the light was on. This
same incident happened a third time. I quoted to him from
Jesus: "I am the light of the world." I said to him, "God is
showing himself to you."

This man became so motivated that he read the entire
New Testament in one day and one night. Before long, I
was able to baptize him.

One day he showed me a picture of a famous radical
Muslim. I recognized the figure, for I knew I had seen that
face before. He said he worked for that man as a spy. After
the United States 9/11 attack, I saw that the Muslim man he
worked for was famous indeed. The very first Muslim I led
to Christ in that new country was someone who worked for
Osama bin Laden.

Many others had dreams and visions like this man. It was very common. For me, it was easy to lead a Muslim to Jesus. I wouldn't talk about converting at all. I merely told them about Jesus. I would just show them the love of Jesus. I didn't worry about them changing their religion.

Then many persecuted believers came to the country. The media had exposed the efforts of Christianity in Iraq, and now the Christians were facing hardship because of it. Soon after that, the officials began to realize that I was doing ministry and training church leaders. Once again I was put in prison, together with a friend. While in prison, we saw another mission field. We were contested many times by many Muslims, but we still shared the love of Jesus. And many of them shared their dreams and visions of Jesus with us.

Since then, I have been in many countries, always ministering to the Arab world and helping to share the love of Jesus. 💬

You know what strikes me the most about Andrew's story? It's the way he boldly and tirelessly preached the gospel, even when it resulted in prison time. And he didn't stop there. Prison became his new mission field! Rather than prison being a punishment, Andrew saw it as a further opportunity to boldly proclaim the gospel. To Andrew, it wasn't the authorities who put him there; rather, it was God!

Andrew is compelled to preach wherever he goes. You can

almost hear the urgent words of Paul on his lips: "How can they hear about [Jesus] unless someone tells them?" (Romans 10:14, NLT).

He doesn't assume that someone else must be taking care of spreading the gospel. Because he follows Jesus, he believes it is his responsibility to share the story of Jesus with others.

It's all because the gospel means something to him. And this causes me to wonder about us. What does the gospel mean to us? What does the Good News of Jesus' life, death, resurrection, and ascension actually mean to us if we're unwilling to share the love and message of Jesus with others?

Sometimes we say we're afraid or feel inadequate. We're hesitant to interrupt the lives of other people or to chance offending them. We rationalize our way out of it, and yet we find our persecuted brothers and sisters unwilling to indulge such thinking, even though it often costs them far more to speak.

It's simple to them. "Jesus loved us, he died for us, and he has saved us. Then he told us to love our neighbors." How could they actually love their neighbors if they withheld the most important news in the world from them? They truly believe Jesus is the hope their neighbors are looking for!

Sharing Jesus almost always costs them something, and in some parts of the world, it might even cost them their lives. Yet they embrace the risk and move into the pain of the unknown, declaring, "Even though I walk through the valley of the shadow of death, I will fear no evil, for you are with me" (Psalm 23:4, ESV).

If the statistics are to be believed, in the free church—where most of us don't fear for our lives—many of us tell hardly anyone about Jesus. We're content to hoard Jesus' forgiveness for ourselves. We're grateful for our hope and for our salvation, but then we make a thousand excuses why we don't share that Good News with others.

Andrew's story should inspire each of us to boldly proclaim the gospel, because it illustrates that preaching is not just for preachers; it's for anyone who follows Jesus. It's about sharing Jesus' Good News wherever God has placed us.

It's convicting, isn't it?

I know my own heart. I'm not sure I would have had Jesus on my mind in prison, where my focus would have been on myself and my problems. And I certainly would not have been eager to preach the gospel immediately after being freed from prison. I probably would have taken some time off and gotten back to my faith in a little while. I'd want to take a vacation and recover.

But not Andrew. He views each setback and success as a further opportunity to spread the Good News about Jesus.

Sometimes we think that sharing the gospel is the responsibility of the professionals, pastors, and priests. Yet Andrew's story dispels that myth. The greatest evangelists among persecuted Christians around the world aren't the professionals. They're the prisoners and parents, sons and daughters and shop owners. While we might expect God's trusted servants to look and act like SEAL Team Six, they often appear on the surface to be quite normal, if not lowly. The heroes you're reading about in these pages have nothing external to distinguish them—except perhaps the marks and aftereffects of their torture. No halo shines over them; no angelic choir can be heard as they speak. They're not the type of people you could never aspire to be. In fact, in most circumstances they've had far less of everything than you and I have enjoyed our entire lives. Sometimes they are very imperfect people with their own flaws and sins.

And as they live out their faith, there is no script to tell them how to feel or how things will turn out. The stories I have chosen to share with you leave us all without excuse. There are no supersaints in these pages—just normal, regular people who love Jesus.

Jesus doesn't have to, but he has chosen to use people like them. And like us.

The question is simply whether we love Jesus as they do. If we do, then we will preach the gospel as they do, with the power and help of the Holy Spirit.

Only our God would choose widows to stare down dictators, orphans to overcome generals, and prisoners to topple tyrants. Yet that's exactly what he's doing. As a great teacher from a bygone age once noted, "He sent not kings and philosophers to persuade fishermen, but fishermen to convert philosophers and kings. They that had no authority to countenance them, no friends to side them, no oratory to second them, no riches to maintain them."[2]

A movement that started with twelve regular guys in an upper room in Jerusalem has become the largest and fastest-growing religion in the world today. Andrew's story—and countless others like it—force us to grapple with an uncomfortable question: How can we take Jesus' peace for ourselves and so easily keep that peace from others by our silence and indifference? How could we stand with a life preserver in our arms while others drown in front of us?

Part of what it means to take the Martyr's Oath is to be willing to boldly preach Jesus in whatever circumstances God places us—even when they are uncomfortable or dangerous. But when we truly believe that Jesus gave his life for us, we, like Andrew, will be compelled to proclaim him wherever we are and wherever we go.

And when we don't, we'll feel our consciences crying out to us. I'm concerned that too often we don't even know how to hear that quiet voice anymore.

How will they know if we do not tell them?

# WHETHER IN ABUNDANCE OR NEED, IN SAFETY OR PERIL, IN PEACE OR DISTRESS, I WILL NOT KEEP QUIET

*I know how to live on almost nothing or with everything. I have learned the secret of living in every situation, whether it is with a full stomach or empty, with plenty or little. For I can do everything through Christ, who gives me strength.*

PHILIPPIANS 4:12-13, NLT

**I HAVE TO CONFESS** that for those of us in affluent countries, this statement from the Martyr's Oath can be difficult to fully comprehend. The reason is that, for many of us, it is so foreign to our experience. We can too easily avoid experiences like "need," "peril," and "distress." Our governments provide safety nets for us, and if we find the right job, the right neighborhood, or the right opportunity, these words are almost removed from our vocabularies altogether. The irony is that, even in our relative ease, many of us have chosen to be silent about our faith. You would think that we would be more bold with so few challenges and so little opposition. Yet according to a recent LifeWay Research study, while 80 percent of churchgoing

Christians believe it is necessary to tell others about Jesus, less than 40 percent have done so in the last six months.[1]

Contrast this with the apostle Paul, whose letter to the Philippians was written from jail. Paul, while in prison for preaching the gospel, was looking for more opportunities to preach—even if it led to his death! Paul's famous statement that "I can do everything through Christ, who gives me strength" is given in the context of contentment amid persecution. The strength Paul experiences through Christ is the strength to endure every circumstance. Contentment in Christ makes living "on almost nothing" like living "with everything." This is made even more clear by the tone and theme of Paul's prison letter to the church at Philippi. He doesn't write in sorrow or anguish. The theme of the letter is *joy*! His mission was endowed with a supernatural power that helped him find the silver lining around every dark cloud.

And this brings us to the story of Peter.

### PETER  || *China*

*Tall and handsome, articulate and intelligent, Peter looks like the young man every father hopes his daughter will one day meet. So it's surprising to learn he is older. Peter looks young, perhaps because he exudes enthusiasm and his face explodes with joy. Animated, talkative, and friendly, Peter seems lit from within by a bright fire.*

*When Peter was ten years old, he witnessed his witch-doctor grandmother have a life-changing encounter with Jesus. Then he*

*made a decision to follow Jesus and dedicated himself to witness
to everyone around him.*

*The first real persecution Peter faced was at his university,
where he was pressured to renounce his faith or step down
from student leadership. But it was his later imprisonment that
marked him. He tells each piece of his story earnestly, rapidly.
He stops to laugh, wipes his eyes. Then tells the next part, stops
to laugh, wipes his eyes. But the more he repeats the process,
the more you sense that some of those tears are not mere humor.
Some tears reflect painful memories, and others are out of deep
gratitude for what God has done for him and for the persecuted
church he serves.*

    "I had been baptized as a boy when Watchman Nee's teams
came to do ministry.[2] At that time, my grandma was a
high-ranking witch in a witchcraft coven. She could per-
form miraculous signs. She would "heal" people, but then
she would take on the suffering of those she was healing.
She would get sick herself, and our family would also suffer from disease or from our animals dying. Grandma grew
frustrated and fearful. She had a special room in her house
to worship idols. The atmosphere was very dark in there.
All of my family was afraid to go near there.

    During that time, many evangelists started traveling to
our town. One day, two evangelists came to my house and
prayed for my grandma. She heard that when you believe
in Jesus, he brings peace and blessing to your life. So she
accepted Jesus as her Savior. Then the evangelists burned
all of Grandma's idols. I will never forget coming home

from school that day. Immediately, I felt like there was light in our house.

But there were still evil spirits in Grandma. So the evangelists continually came to our home to lay hands on her and cast out evil spirits. My grandma was possessed! When they would pray for her, she would scream. I know it was the evil spirits speaking. Then suddenly one day she was fine! The evil spirits were gone!

I have three sisters. We were little kids watching this unfold. I came to trust Jesus after I saw such a dramatic change. I knew there was a God, and that God had the power to defeat evil!

After all of this, a peace filled our home. I was filled with joy. I led my mother to the Lord. Soon all of my family was saved. I would read the Bible secretly, even in school, right up until I finished college. I prayed a lot. It didn't matter what I encountered, I would pray. Persecution began. Yet there were also signs and wonders that accompanied our lives.

At university, I felt the Lord was preparing to teach me some hard lessons. Before, I was just a new Christian, and now the Lord started to ask me to sacrifice some things. The first year I was at university, I became class president. But one weekend, my professor couldn't find me. He was a Communist Party member. Only my best friend knew where I was. The professor found him. My friend told him that I was at church. The professor was furious. When I came back from church, he said, "You are a youth being raised under the red flag of the Communist Party, so you should not indulge yourself with Western thoughts and religion."

Then came other school leaders and Communist Party leaders. They all tried to lead me away from Christian thinking. But I prayed constantly through all of this, and the Lord strengthened me.

Finally, my professor threatened me. He said I could give up my Christian beliefs or give up being class president. I told my professor that I would rather be a Christian than head of the class. He thought that was unbelievable. Why would anyone make this kind of sacrifice for Jesus? But I felt free and relieved. As class president, I couldn't tell others I was a Christian or I'd be removed, but now I could share Jesus freely with my friends on campus.

After college, I wasn't completely satisfied in my heart, because I saw many people come to church for different purposes. Some people wanted blessings for their business. Others wanted to find relationships. I was disappointed with these attitudes. I wanted a more authentic spiritual life and to become more mature in my faith.

So I cried out, "If you're a God that exists just to meet people's needs, then I don't want to believe in you anymore. If you want me to continuously follow you, give me direction as to which way I should go in my life."

That year, there was a Christian leadership conference south of my area. I went because I wanted to become a church leader. But at this conference, many of us were arrested. Thirty or forty elders and people in leadership were brought to prison.

The officials thought I was a top leader because I was well educated. They placed me in a solitary room. They watched me minute by minute. The police asked the head of the prison, the big boss, to monitor me closely. Then the guards began to beat me.

I was young and afraid. But then came the day they asked me to share about Christianity. And it was the big boss who said all the prisoners were required to listen as well!

"Everyone, listen carefully," the big boss said. "If he repeats himself, you can beat him." The prison had a rule that we had to study in the morning and evening. But now they had to study by listening to me teach about Christianity!

I would preach twice a day, starting from Genesis without a Bible. I touched on nearly everything, especially why we need Jesus. After each session, the big boss would debate with me. I had to pretend he would win. But I knew that every time I would preach, hearts were softening.

There was hierarchy within the jail. Originally, I had to clean toilets, but every day after I would preach, I would get upgraded. Soon I was moved to a wooden bed. Then I got to sleep near the big boss, not near the toilets. Finally I started to get meat sometimes, not just a little rice. So I knew the big boss was slowly changing his mind.

The big boss was a kung fu master. He could beat anyone. He had restless hands. Any disobedience was met with his wrath. And he had a law degree. After I stayed there one month, he said, "You must be sentenced to at least three years!"

That's when I cried out to God, "Lord, I can't be here three years!" Then I prayed, "Lord, if I bring this man to Christ, then can I go?" The presence of the Lord was so real, so strong! All I could do was continue to pray. Then I felt relaxed and released by God.

One night, the big boss couldn't sleep. He asked me to talk to him. He said one of my words from God touched him. He began to open up. He told me he came from a celebrity family and was the head of the mafia in another city. He was part of the "Black Society," with three thousand subordinates under him. "Even the mayor would kneel to me and submit to me," he said.

"Everyone was afraid of me," he said. He was also a high-ranking officer. But when he was stationed at that prison, everyone ignored him, "even my wife and children."

He started telling me his secrets. One night, he said he thought I'd be transferred to another jail, or maybe even released. Suddenly he said, "So we have no time left. What can I do to be saved?" I led him to Christ that night. After the big boss received Christ, he changed! In the past, every day he felt he had to beat someone. But now, when he would get provoked, he'd say, "If it weren't for Christ, I would beat you!"

All of the people in that cell were saved! Fifteen people total!

The big boss asked me, "Besides confessing my sins, what else do I need to do?"

I said, "You need to be baptized." We didn't know how to do that in the jail. But then we decided there was a small tank in the shower for bathing that we could use. One day, we stepped outside to get some fresh air, and the big boss said, "Okay, let's do it now."

We filled the tank in the shower, and when he came out of the water, he was so joyful. He was ecstatic. He ran to tell the others there that he had been saved!

The very next day, I got the news that I was released. Right before I left, the big boss asked me questions, like how to pray. I only had a little time, so I wrote down some verses for him. Ever since then, I have been in ministry. God has protected me. 🙶

Peter didn't press pause on his faith when his faith put him in prison. Peter would not keep quiet. On the contrary, the more others turned up the heat, the more he preached. The fact is that when Christianity is under pressure, the church often grows rather than declines. The same is true in our own individual lives. When we are put under pressure, we grow too.

This might seem counterintuitive. You would think that when we have peace, we would be more likely to be thankful to God and to make him the center of our lives. But listen to what Moses told the Israelites when they were about to enter the Promised Land:

The LORD your God is bringing you into a good land of flowing streams and pools of water, with fountains and springs that gush out in the valleys and hills. . . . But that is the time to be careful! Beware that in your plenty you do

JOHNNIE MOORE || 43

not forget the LORD your God and disobey his commands, regulations, and decrees that I am giving you today.

DEUTERONOMY 8:7, 11, NLT

Moses warned the Israelites that they would be in *greater* danger when they entered the Promised Land than they were in the wilderness. What a warning for us today, especially those of us who live in places like the United States!

We are in greater spiritual danger when we're in abundance, safety, and peace than when we're in need, peril, or distress. Most of us barely realize it, and this is why our faith is so weak.

The worst sins that derail our Christian life are just what John lists: "the lust of the flesh, the lust of the eyes, and the pride of life" (1 John 2:16). And these are abundant in the safety and security of the West. Our prosperity allows us to sin without feeling the consequences of it in the egregious forms these consequences take in other parts of the world. Because sin's consequences seem under control, we convince ourselves that we don't need Jesus. We might not openly admit that, but that's how we live. We might as well be living as if he doesn't exist at all!

When we have a roof over our heads, money in the bank, a car to get around, or a good education, we don't feel in our hearts as if we need Jesus as much. We instead just run to him when we need something from him. We treat him like a genie in a bottle.

The persecuted church doesn't have such a luxury. They need Jesus every single day, and they experience him in an entirely different way.

As strange as it sounds, from what I've seen, it's sometimes easier to live boldly for Jesus when Jesus is your only hope, when he's all you have. And I think that's why the testimony of Christianity is so brilliant in the worst darkness. It speaks to a power that transcends our world's challenges.

What encourages me about Peter's story and about the stories of so many other believers around the world is that many of these people have comparatively nothing, and they simply do not need anything more. Meanwhile, we are so often obsessed with more, more, more—more of anything, more of everything!

This is why believers imprisoned for Jesus are often freer than those of us who have been afforded the luxury of excess. They get thrown into prisons; we build our own, walling ourselves in with our material possessions and boxing up our hearts with our greed. Eventually we can barely feel our faith anymore, while our persecuted brothers and sisters have only their faith to feel.

Whether Peter was a class leader at the university or holed up in jail, he was content with Jesus alone. Faith like his is a challenge to all of us, forcing us to reconsider what we're doing to live for the Jesus whom believers like Peter are willing to die for.

So how do we identify with our suffering brothers and sisters around the world? How do we find the faith they have when we don't face the challenges they face?

The answer is simple to say but hard to live: we must find empathy with them.

Empathy is the experience of feeling what others feel. It means we climb into their flesh and bones; we put our feet in their shoes, our minds in their minds, and we imagine what it would be like to be them.

This is one of the most difficult things for Western Christians.

Their experience isn't ours, so in order to understand it, in order to find empathy, we have to be intentional.

We must use our imaginations to put ourselves in the dark and difficult places around the world, where war and poverty and injustice are so common. We must see in superabundant form that the evil on our planet is all rooted in the same sin that tempts us to be prideful or to be materialistic or to break any one of God's commandments.

Our natural tendency is to want to avoid discomfort and suffering, and so if we're not invested in the lives of our Christian brothers and sisters around the world, it's all too easy to change the channel or filter the news to our liking.

But that isn't what we're called to do. The author of Hebrews says we are to "remember those in prison, as if you were there yourself" (Hebrews 13:3, NLT).

Then, our empathy leads us to action. Not just in our own hearts, but with our hands and our feet. Paul writes in his letter to the Galatians that "whenever we have the opportunity, we should do good to everyone—especially to those in the family of faith" (6:10, NLT). Christians should be the first ones lending aid in any crisis, but especially in a crisis that involves our fellow Christians. In order to know and help our brothers and sisters, we have to fight our inclination to shelter ourselves from what's going on in the world. Because once we know them, we can no longer remain silent.

Rather than run away from the difficult situations around the world—and difficult is an understatement—we must run toward these challenges. But we will run toward our suffering family only if we run away from all the forms of materialism that attempt to wall us off from contentment in our own heart. We cannot shut our eyes and close our ears any longer.

When there's a crisis in the world, Christians do not shield themselves from it. And when we watch the evening news or listen to the radio or read on the Internet and learn that there's conflict in the Congo or the Sudan or in Syria, we mustn't turn away. We mustn't filter our social media or skip those uncomfortable reports. We have a moral obligation as God's hands and feet to know what's happening so we can know how to help. We should be asking ourselves, *As a light of the world, what light am I to shine in this?*

Abundance can be a gift. In fact, many times throughout Scripture, God placed people in positions of wealth or influence in order to bring about his purposes, and surely he does so now. But abundance can also be a distraction and an excuse. We will never serve and love as we must until we find contentment in abundance or need, in safety or peril, in peace or distress.

# CHAPTER 5

# HIS UNFAILING LOVE
# IS BETTER THAN LIFE

*The LORD is my light and my salvation—whom shall I fear?*
*The LORD is the stronghold of my life—of whom shall I be afraid?*

PSALM 27:1

**WE HAVE SEEN JIHADISTS CRUCIFY CHRISTIANS**, behead Christians, put Christians in cages and drown them, burn elderly Christian women alive, and execute Christians en masse. And far from doing these things in the dark of night, these terrorists film it all, edit it into slick videos, and use these horrifying acts as recruiting tools. Social media and the Internet have become their Roman Coliseum, displaying their atrocities to the entire world. On the day I'm writing these words, it happened twice.

And while the territory controlled by ISIS has shrunk in the Middle East from its height in 2014, their ideology continues to inspire attacks around the world and spread to other countries, like Egypt and Libya. Their tactics are also changing, and now they are sending their radical recruits back to the West to attempt to commit the same kinds of acts here. Between October 2014 and the summer of 2016, there were eight ISIS-inspired attacks in North America (*not including* the bombings perpetrated by Ahmad Khan Rahami in New York and New Jersey in September 2016) and eighteen in Europe.[1] In nations like France, this leaves many citizens worried, sometimes afraid to leave their houses, afraid to live their lives.

Former FBI director James Comey acknowledged nearly nine hundred open investigations of ISIS sympathizers who are in all fifty states in the United States.[2]

The terrorists may seem powerful, confident, and on the offensive but in fact *none* of these things is true. Here's what is true:

- The territory they control is becoming progressively smaller.
- The number of people they control is becoming progressively smaller.
- The number of Christians converting from Islam is becoming progressively larger.
- The tactics they employ have marginalized them even more, especially within Islamic societies, where the vast majority of people eschew violence.
- The bravado of "We love death more than you love life" is nothing more than an attempt to mask the hole in their souls that only the true God can fill. It's one big lie.

How do we know the bravado is a facade? Because once these men and women are free from legal restrictions and family and peer pressure and once they are allowed to seek the truth for themselves, they are coming to faith in Jesus in unprecedented numbers. In the meantime, that isn't stopping Jesus from going after them where they are. There are countless stories emerging from the Middle East of supernatural conversions through dreams and visions of Jesus.

The barbarity and indiscriminate nature of ISIS's atrocities are evidence of their desperation, just as the strength of Christians in response to these heinous acts is evidence of the power of the gospel and of the unfailing love of Jesus. There is a love stronger than fear.

## SAMI || *Iraq*

*Sami is in full-time ministry, distributing Bibles to refugees in Europe. Holding a Bible is still a thrill for him. He lived through the first harrowing months of his Christian faith without even having seen one.*

*On a hot, dusty day, Sami set out with his friends, all in their thirties, to drive the hundred miles from Baghdad to An-Najaf. Their destination was the ancient walled city that boasted the important Shia shrine to Ali. A new international airport and huge sports stadium now shared the landscape with the shrine's gold dome and towers, the rest of the city a mix of ancient and modern buildings.*

*As the modern city streets and buildings of Baghdad disappeared behind them, the young friends followed the road along the fertile Euphrates River floodplains, then headed southeast into the desert. They took a wrong turn and inadvertently headed farther east. As they watched the road, expecting An-Najaf to come into view, instead a checkpoint loomed. Drawing close, they realized too late that it was no checkpoint. A band of men with guns opened fire.*

" I am thirty-three years old, and I came to Christ by accident.

My friends and I took a wrong turn driving to An-Najaf and went down a road where several armed men surrounded us and started shooting at us. They forced the driver to stop. They took us to a desolate place for three days with our eyes blindfolded. On the third day, they took the blindfolds off. They took us to a place and put us in a row at the edge of a big hole. There they started pushing us and shooting us, one by one.

At the time, I only knew about Jesus from a television series I had watched. I had searched for the name of the series, and to my astonishment, I found out that it was produced in Iran! It was the story of followers of Christ who were persecuted and ran to hide in a cave.

Standing at the edge of that hole, I knew it was the last moment of my life, so I started to pray what I had heard on television: "I love you, Jesus. Have mercy on me and forgive me." How great is our God! He used a television series produced by Iranians to bring me to Christ.

The gunmen shot the man next to me, and his blood covered my face. Then came my turn. I kept praying inside. One of the men pushed me into the big hole, and the other man began shooting at me a series of bullets. It was a game to them. But in a miraculous way, they all missed me.

Their game continued, and the corpses of other men fell over me. One of the gunmen shouted, "Someone is still alive." So they started shooting at me again, but the corpse above me protected me. They thought I was dead.

The gunmen went to bring some shovels to bury us. I lay there for hours, and they didn't return. Dark came, so I rose up, all covered with blood, and went to a river and washed myself. I walked to the main road with the name of Christ on my tongue all the way.

When I got home, people around me learned about my faith in Christ, so I became their enemy. I didn't know why. My father was ready to kill me if he saw me. He even gave my name to the militiamen to kill me. I went to many churches, but none of them would accept me. They were all afraid. I had to run away.

I went from place to place, hiding. They caught me and put me in the cellar of an Islamic court. I thought it might be the end of my life. I knew there is a great God, and some people are ready to die for his sake, so I was ready too.

I was hung from my hands for three days from the ceiling of a tomb. I was tortured for fifteen days by brutal instruments. I was shocked by electricity many times until I fainted. I was covered with blood and left lying in that tomb filled with insects. The guards kept asking me to recant and promised to give me everything I could dream of if I renounced Jesus.

I refused to leave my faith, so they sentenced me to death. I said, "If you are going to kill me, I would like to

die like Christ, on a cross." They prepared a cross for me
and were going to crucify me the next day.

That last night, while I lay on the ground, I felt some
drops of water falling on me. It was coming from an opening in the ceiling. That opening was covered by a network
of wires. I pushed myself up and tried to reach the opening. I was surprised to see the wires were rusting because
of the water! I easily pushed them aside. It was heaven's
door open to me. I pushed myself out of that opening and
ran away.

I crossed the border, where I met some Iraqi young
men and traveled by boat with them. On the way, there
were waves in the sea that were very high. I called upon
the name of Jesus. When the others heard me, they
shoved me into the sea. I didn't know how to swim, and
the waves were pushing me for three hours toward the
shore. Where I landed, the police came and picked me
up out of the water.

Three times I was saved from death. I am sure that
Jesus is the one who saved me. I should have been a dead
person like the others. Even if they cut me into a thousand
pieces, I will never leave him. 🙶

When Sami's life seemed to be at its end, he reached out to Jesus,
and Jesus spared him. But Sami didn't leave it there. Rather, his cry
out to Jesus in desperation changed the whole course of his life.
And that decision was made at great personal cost.

Sami reminds us that Jesus' love is better than life, and his commitment to Jesus was a testimony of his love to everyone who aimed to kill him. Sami lived Jesus' teaching that "anyone who loves their life will lose it, while anyone who hates their life in this world will keep it for eternal life" (John 12:25).

Sami's willingness to die for the love of Christ isn't unique. It's the experience of countless Christians around the world. But is it *our* experience? If not, do we truly comprehend the love of God? Do we see its unfailing power, and are we so moved by it that we would be willing to sacrifice at all for it, much less offer the ultimate sacrifice—our lives?

For Sami, he didn't just serve Jesus. He loved him. Jesus' love compelled him.

Stop for a moment. Look in your heart. How deeply moved are you by the love of Jesus? Does it touch you, or have you become too accustomed to it, too used to his story?

In Luke 7, Jesus says to Simon the Pharisee that our willingness to love others is in direct proportion to our own experience of the love of God. The apostle John puts it even more bluntly: "Whoever does not love does not know God, because God is love. . . . We love because he first loved us" (1 John 4:8, 19).

Our love for others is a direct outflow of God's love within us.

For Sami, God's love was all new, and it was literally his salvation. For many of us, it sometimes feels old, and we simply use Jesus as a kind of ticket to heaven. Jesus didn't die on the cross simply to give us a ticket to heaven. He died on the cross because we were powerless to repair our relationship with God. He took it all on the chin for us so that we can spend eternity with God—starting now.

Maybe this all sounds a bit ethereal to you, a bit too theological or philosophical. So let me get down to brass tacks: What does it mean that Jesus' unfailing love is better than life?

One of the clearest examples is what happened in Rome in AD 165 and 250. When a plague hit the city, the plutocrats left immediately, leaving their fellow citizens to die in the streets. But the Christians, encouraged by their leaders, stayed in the city to minister to the dying and to ensure that the dead received a proper and dignified burial. This was still a time of persecution and a time of suffering. Yet the Christians served some of those who would have otherwise persecuted them. The Christians willingly sacrificed their own lives in service of those who would never do the same for them and might have preferred the Christians imprisoned—or worse.

Many Christians therefore caught the plague themselves, but they considered the love of God as expressed to others of greater value than their own lives. One of the interesting side effects of this decision was that, while many Christians died in the plague, others survived because they developed immunity through their service.

I see in this a lesson for all of us today.

While it is natural and in many ways understandable to avoid danger, God provides the greatest blessings when we risk it all on love, when we run into desperate situations and witness the love of God to others. Again, as Jesus said, "Anyone who loves their life will lose it, while anyone who hates their life in this world will keep it for eternal life."

Brother Andrew, the famous Bible smuggler and founder of Open Doors International, is fond of saying that he has only one regret in his ministry. Andrew wishes he would have taken more risks!

Why?

Because God's love requires a radical life.

It means that whatever it costs and however another person might reciprocate, we choose to love anyway. God's love isn't just for people who love us. It's for people who hate us too. We choose to love others because we love him more than we love our lives on this earth.

Consider when Christian widows in Egypt chose to love and forgive the ISIS butchers who beheaded their husbands in 2015, stating as much in the national Egyptian newspapers.

When something like that happens, we're all just flabbergasted. We're stopped in our tracks. It's because it's so rare for us to see this supernatural love manifested so profoundly. Yet it should be something much more commonplace in a world with two billion people who profess to follow Jesus Christ.

Love is *just what Christians do*. But instead, we're as surprised as anyone else when such extravagant love shows up among our own. And so before we can reach the vision of love the Bible tells us we ought to have, we must begin walking in love—perhaps slowly, plodding, taking baby steps while we learn what it means to walk this way.

You walk in love with the coworker who treats you unfairly or the person who trolls you on the Internet. You walk in love with that person who has something against you or who did something terrible to you.

You walk in love. You take a thousand different steps, all in the same direction, until you become a person of love, so immersed in the experience of Jesus' sacrifice that love becomes who you are and not just something you do.

That's when love changes you.

But remember—true love shows up only when it costs you

something. And to truly, deeply, radically love others, we must first experience the love of God ourselves.

Many Christians who are facing desperate persecution are forgiving their oppressors. Their actual experiences are varied, but they are united by their belief that "Jesus' unfailing love is better than life."

The love of Jesus compels them. It sustains them. It is their greatest witness. Perhaps we experience so little love because our expectations are way too high. We expect love to be a gift to *us*, but love was always meant to be a gift to *others*—a gift most valuable when given in exchange for hate. Love that causes forgiveness breaks through hardened hearts and shows a path to salvation for those imprisoned by the darkest forms of hatred.

# CHAPTER 6

# HIS GRACE COMPELS ME TO SPEAK HIS NAME EVEN IF HIS NAME COSTS ME EVERYTHING

*Christ's love compels us, because we are convinced that one died for all, and therefore all died. And he died for all, that those who live should no longer live for themselves but for him who died for them and was raised again.*

2 CORINTHIANS 5:14-15

**THE BIBLE IS THE MOST BURNED BOOK** in the world, and the most banned. It's the most loved and the most despised, and there aren't books large enough to contain the stories of those who have attempted to extinguish it from our world.

The story of persecution you will read in this chapter begins with Ermias's desire to simply know and study the Bible. His story isn't unusual, as Christians all over the world face imprisonment for simply owning or studying this book. Some jihadists have even been reported to use pages of Bibles for toilet paper.[1] Others have chosen to keep a copy for themselves—hidden to read under the dark of night—and their curiosity has eventually led them to faith.

Brave believers cherish this book. The printed Bible itself is the product of countless martyrs, and today the Book of Life still costs some followers of Jesus their own lives. Yet that living book has transcended every effort to stamp it out.

The reason why so many persecutors are against the Bible is that they view it as a threat. The Bible is God's "inside language" to our conscience. The Bible says the Word is written on and hidden in our hearts, so when we read it, God is sending a message in his own language directly to the deepest part of us. And it *is* a threat to any ideology that opposes it. It's a threat to political leaders who don't want people to think for themselves. It's a threat to the enemy, who doesn't want us to know the truth. It's no coincidence that the most tyrannical regimes in history have always banned religion and specifically Christianity and the Bible. This book has caused men and women not only to know what is right but also to recognize their own free will, designed by God. And free will is a threat to tyranny.

The fact is that love for the Bible is often where persecution begins. The Bible is a book that changes people, and it threatens our own attempts to maintain charge of our lives, and it threatens those who want to control other people. The Bible puts God in his rightful place, and us in ours.

Yet the truth of the Bible will not—cannot—be silenced, and Jesus' followers through the ages have given everything in love for God's Word.

This is how it all began for Ermias.

## ERMIAS || *Ethiopia*

*A Whitney Houston song blares from the speakers of the restaurant. The clanging kitchen, the roaring whoosh of trucks passing outside, and the smell of food punctuated by the thick aroma of coffee all create an unsettling atmosphere. But Ermias is unfazed. He's focused on telling his story, which feels like it could be a continuation of the book of Acts. He's well educated and fluent in many languages. He speaks concisely, fluidly, earnestly, relaying events from almost two decades in a rapid-fire pattern, as if it's all just part of his march to spread the gospel.*

*Ermias is a native Ethiopian, light-skinned, short, and a little overweight, with a sculpted beard. He stands out. He looks like he could be a foreigner, from almost anywhere. And that is what has saved his life. Security couldn't peg him in the many countries where he's lived and traveled. Security also found they couldn't stop him.*

*Whatever nationality he may seem to be, Ermias is an on-fire Christian. He is passionate about his faith and desperate to reach the Arab world—to "change history for God." When told by jailers that he had to convert to Islam, he turned the tables and started a church in their prison. When sent back to Ethiopia as a punishment, he started witnessing to Arab men, leading them to Jesus. He carries photos and videos on his phone of people who received healing and of others who made the decision to follow the faith.*

*The first time he was jailed, he was imprisoned for several months. He was jailed only because he had a hunger for the Bible. The second time, he was caught only because he was riding in a car with an illegal immigrant. That time, after he served time in prison, he was banished from the country. He has faced harrowing ordeals fleeing countries both by sea and by land. He's been robbed, tortured, mocked. He's been everything—except, perhaps, discouraged.*

*Some people might tire of the ministry, the risk of imprisonment, the separation from their families, the harrowing escapes. Ermias and his wife can hardly wait to be reunited, to strike out anew and minister to the Arab world. It's Jesus' grace that compels them, whatever the cost. They almost don't even recognize that it's a "cost" anymore.*

" When I was in high school, I started a Bible correspondence course. I would receive about fifteen or twenty pages of Christian literature at a time, so the letters I got were very thick. The government was cracking down on the church at this time. They noticed my thick letters coming in and put me in prison for months for no reason, just because I had that material.

After several months, a government employee helped get me out. I was born in Ethiopia, so the government ordered me to return to Ethiopia. But the border was closed then, so they said I had to stop learning and just sit in my house. I was not permitted to receive literature or go anywhere.

At that time, church members were being beaten. The government was disbanding churches. Church activities were closed. After a few months, my sister and I paid the equivalent of $350 US to flee on a small boat run by smugglers. About eighty-five immigrants were with us, almost

80 percent of them Ethiopian. The rest were Eritrean. We spent three days and nights on the sea. Not all immigrant boats make it to their destination, and the smugglers are not trustworthy. It was very dangerous.

The area we reached was near a city that was unstable politically. Tribes were clashing. Everybody carried weapons. Because they live on an immigration route, they were all watching for immigrants to rob.

We reached the coast after midnight. We had no water, no food, no compass. Even in the boat, the water was bad. The captain mixed some petrol in the water so it would smell bad and we wouldn't drink much. When we landed, we didn't know where to go. Eighty-five people lost in the dark. We were afraid the local men would take the women for sex, so we divided into two groups to protect the women. We started walking. We could hear the bark of the desert dogs—the jackals and hyenas.

Soon we saw candlelight, so we sent the group of men toward it, hoping to find people who might have food and water. Instead, we encountered gunshots. The people took our money, our watches, our shoes. They gave us water, but it was mixed with camel urine, considered to have medicinal properties. This was the desert, very hot, and we were so thirsty, so even this water tasted good to us.

The desert dogs kept barking and howling, so the men pointed their guns at us and said, "There are more of you. They are making the dogs bark." They went out and found our other group and took all of their possessions. They robbed the girls even but didn't touch them.

After they robbed us, they were going to let us go, but we said, "Where will we go?" One of them was kind and said, "Follow that one star to get to the border." Then our groups divided. The group my sister and I were in had about eighteen people. I never saw any of the other people again.

My group started walking. We were weak, but we walked for a few hours. When we needed rest, we found a mountain with a cave and slept there. As we slept, some young men followed our tracks on their motorbikes. They rode around the mountain for a long time, but they couldn't find where we went, so they left.

We woke up at sunrise. In the distance, we saw camels, so we walked toward them and found a house. We asked the people in the house for water, a mother and her daughter. The mother said, "Tell your brother to come." We didn't know it, but she was calling for her son and his friends with machine guns to rob us! We hoped to get water, but when the son came, they took us outside and robbed us again. We were already robbed and didn't have anything, so they took a lot of our clothes.

Finally, we walked all the way to a town closer to the next border—almost forty miles. We met a man watering one hundred and fifty camels outside of town. He allowed us to drink and wash from his well.

We set off again that night, but the sand was soft. It was not easy to walk, because our legs would sink. After about an hour, we heard the wind come. It was strong. We couldn't go into any city, so we had to stay out there in the desert. Then rain started. We hardly had any clothes. We had no food. We were very weak, and we didn't know where to go, so we just sat down under a tree. The jackals and hyenas smelled us and came barking, but we stayed safe. That was the worst night. The next morning, some kind people came. They put us in a very old car, and they took us near the border.

We walked the rest of the way. Soldiers with machine guns and official cars were everywhere. There are many trafficked girls on that road, so it is heavily guarded, but we had no choice. We had to cross that border. When we came to the gate, the border guards stopped us. We asked them for water. They gave us water out of bottles in their car. We told them we were Ethiopians and just wanted to get to Ethiopia. We said we would just transition through their country, not stay there. They let us through, but they warned us that there might be special forces inside who would arrest us for being illegal.

Once inside this new country, we found our brother who lived there legally. I stayed with him for eight months and finished high school. I became fluent in the new language. I became a member of Christ the King Church and married my wife. The leaders asked me to go preach in two towns in the south. I knew those two southern cities were dangerous. There are human traffickers, drug traffickers, weapons traffickers. Also, the church members are mostly illegal immigrants. But I felt God told me to go help them. I took my wife and we moved there.

I prayed that God would help me proclaim his name,

help me be a good brother to the church, a good husband. When we got there, it was difficult to find a place to have a service, and it's also illegal to ask people to come. But the first night I preached, eight people came to believe the teaching about Jesus. Praise God!

The illegals there had to hustle to live. They would go from house to house and sell clothing. They were garden workers, shepherds. I was proud to work with such people who had no education but were so happy to hear about God. They had no money, of course. The church could not support me. But I believed we were changing history and God would take care of us.

The distance between the two churches where I ministered was about fifty kilometers, more than thirty miles. Somehow we would always get the money to go back and forth. Fortunately, I was never stopped by security. I was careful. I wore white like a Muslim. I could speak fluently in every Middle Eastern language. Security couldn't tell what nationality I was.

One day, I was riding from one city to the other with a church member. Police stopped and asked for our IDs. I gave them mine, but the man from our church didn't have an ID. He was illegal. I told them the illegal man was my son, and that's what saved him. All they did was send him back to Ethiopia. But they put me in jail for a long time.

It was a very bad jail. I hadn't seen such a place in my life. It was very dark, small, and crowded. Around 1,350 prisoners share one block. They were all from Middle

East and Asian countries, and they were divided because of their culture, prejudice, religion, so there was always fighting inside the jail.

After about a month, I started to preach in the jail. God gave me power and energy. God gave me two church members right away. First was an Ethiopian. He used to be a Christian, and he prayed with me. The other was an Arab. We discussed the Bible, and I started teaching him about Abraham on up to Jesus. He prayed with us. The jailer who watched us when we prayed would listen. One day I felt I should ask him if he wanted to join us, so he joined us too. More people told me they felt something when we prayed. Then they told other people they felt something. Some Ethiopians went to the Islamic leader and told them they were converting to Christianity. I was so happy!

The Islamic leaders went to the prison office and told them. The jailers brought me to their office and showed me a three-page document outlining accusations they were making against me for my faith. They asked me if this report was true. I said, "Yes it's all true, because I'm a Christian."

The jailers said, "You need to convert to Islam or face punishment." They said they needed a strong teacher like me to convert to Islam. They promised me money and even said they would let me go free if I would convert. They gave me one day to think about it. When they brought me back in, I told them I didn't change my mind.

Two military men and an Islamic teacher brought me to a small room and started torturing me. The two soldiers held me, and the other person broke my toes. They held my hands and pulled off my fingernails. I was crying in pain. They sent me to a solitary cell. They didn't provide any medical treatment. A day later, they sent me back to my regular cell and said I would have to stay in prison longer. Many times they demanded that I convert. They kept postponing my release date, month after month.

Many jailed people have no court sentence, or they finish their sentence, but the paperwork is disorderly and they have to stay. Many people are beheaded in jail. I felt I had no hope to get out. My hands were shackled. My legs were shackled. But I was praying that it was just a test, that I was imprisoned for the sake of God.

At home, they froze my bank account. The church money was stored in that account, so that tied up the money. My wife found work to support herself. Finally, I was released from jail and sent out of the country. My wife and I want to go to other Arab countries to preach. I can speak and write in other languages. I can minister. I know the Koran, so I can teach Muslims. I have energy to preach to the Arabic people! I am committed to bring the gospel to the Arab world! 💬

Ermias's determination to minister despite what it has cost him reminds me of the advice Jesus gave his followers: "If anyone will not receive you or listen to your words, shake off the dust from your feet when you leave that house or town" (Matthew 10:14, ESV). Jesus was advising the disciples to continue preaching the gospel in the next place. Just keep going.

He was saying, "Don't get your feelings hurt, and don't be discouraged—just keep at it." I fear that for many of us, our skin is too thin. If someone mocks us for our faith—or if there's even the prospect of ridicule—then we choose not to raise our voice. We become closeted Christians.

But Ermias just keeps preaching. There is no cost too high to shut his lips or to discourage him from his call and his mission. He is "compelled" to continue. It isn't an option. It is his privilege and his responsibility. He's so close to Jesus—and his belief in the gospel is so strong—that he's pulled like gravity to the next opportunity to tell someone else about Jesus.

It's not that we aren't familiar with this feeling ourselves. We are compelled by lots of things. We're just not compelled by this one thing.

We ought to look in our own hearts and ask ourselves, What are we willing to do at all costs, whether or not it's easy to do?

I've met people compelled by fame, by fortune, by a dream— even the American dream—and by the opinions of others. They'll do *anything* to get that one thing, to reach that next milestone, and to achieve that single aspiration.

Yet if we really believe that Jesus is the hope of the world, then we must allow ourselves to be pulled, to be compelled, by that *truth*. The grace of Jesus is like a magnet drawing us toward others who need his hope, and it's like a mirror that reminds us every day how much we desperately need Jesus ourselves.

All through the New Testament, Christians are considered

strangers and pilgrims. Jesus, while praying for us, says that we are "not of the world" (John 17:16). In other words, there should be something about us that's different from others, with something different compelling us.

We should have a different motivation than the world around us, as when "those who owned land or houses sold them, brought the money from the sales and put it at the apostles' feet, and it was distributed to anyone who had need" (Acts 4:34-35). As ordinary believers we also ought to be so committed to Christ and his people that we are willing to sacrifice our own comfort for others, especially other believers.

Similarly, there should be something about us that the world can't quite understand. I don't mean that people would think of us as strange or weird but that they would certainly see something different in us.

Instead, we kind of blend in. There's nothing different about us. We are conditioned to think and talk and believe in the way the culture encourages us to think and talk and believe, but we forget that our culture isn't a biblical one.

As Christians, we all ought to feel discontentment here. We ought to feel like this world is not our home. Yet many of us *do* feel at home here, at home in our world and comfortable in what we have.

The grace of Jesus has compelled some Christians in persecuted places to remain where it's difficult, because they don't believe they're supposed to feel "right" there to begin with. God's grace has kept Christians in Syria within a stone's throw of ISIS. It has kept Christians in Communist countries even after multiple imprisonments, and it has kept Christians in Nigeria even as Boko Haram has targeted their communities again and again.

Jesus' grace compels us to share his love, especially when and where it's the hardest to share. It cuts through our desire to live cozy lives. It lowers our expectation that this world somehow owes us something.

So how do we change this part of us?

Sometimes, I think we must choose intentional discomfort.

We need to make ourselves uncomfortable. We must sacrifice a little more than we're comfortable with, risk a little more than we're comfortable with, go to places we're uncomfortable to be in. C. S. Lewis has famously said:

> I do not believe one can settle how much we ought to give. I am afraid the only safe rule is to give more than we can spare. . . . If our charities do not at all pinch or hamper us, I should say they are too small. There ought to be things we should like to do and cannot do because our charities expenditure excludes them.[2]

The costs for our faith involve sacrifices—"instead ofs." For some of us, maybe that means instead of giving 10 percent, we give 15 percent. Or instead of taking a mission trip to a relatively stable place like South Africa, we take a mission trip to the Middle East. Maybe instead of going over spring break, we go over Christmas break, taking the whole family with us. There are lots of things we can do to become intentionally uncomfortable, and it will look different for each of us. But if we aren't sacrificing something, then we aren't experiencing faith in Jesus.

And then there's that book that sits on a dusty shelf, leaving our hearts unkempt. That book that calls us to live differently and to love differently and to sacrifice more than what we're comfortable sacrificing. The Bible is the ultimate guide to living differently, and it takes us to a place we desperately need to go. It makes us who we know we need to become. And we cannot find our way without it.

That beautiful book—that banned and burned book—seems to have cost Ermias everything, but it has given him what everyone else in the world seems to be looking for: peace.

# CHAPTER 7

# EVEN IN THE FACE OF DEATH, I WILL NOT DENY HIM

*Simon Peter replied, "Lord, to whom would we go?*
*You have the words that give eternal life. We believe,*
*and we know you are the Holy One of God."*

JOHN 6:68-69, NLT

**I'VE CHOSEN TO RELATE SEVERAL STORIES** about Eritrea in this book, not only because of the bravery of the believers there and the severity of the persecution, not only because Eritrea is little known in the West, but also because it has been termed "the North Korea of Africa" by the US Commission on International Religious Freedom.[1]
One newspaper adds:

Limitations on freedom of movement are just the tip of the iceberg in this East African country that is among the harshest dictatorships in the world. The group Reporters Without Borders ranks the place 179th among 179 countries when it comes to freedom of expression, even lower than North Korea itself.

One of the most glaring reflections of the harshness of the regime in Asmara, the Eritrean capital, is the mandatory military service that citizens on average serve from age 18 until they are 55 and which has spurred many to flee. A spokeswoman for Amnesty International in Israel notes that in a country where the average life expectancy is 61 or 62, this means many spend their entire adult lives in the army, frequently facing hard labor and meager wages.[2]

The Eritrean government officially recognizes Christianity in its law.[3] But don't assume that government recognition means freedom of religion. *The Christian Science Monitor* reports:

Civic space for the free and peaceful practice of religion is incredibly restricted, with the government grossly interfering with Eritrea's four recognized religious communities—the Coptic Orthodox Church, Sunni Islam, Roman Catholicism, and a Lutheran-connected denomination. It has kept Orthodox Patriarch Abune Antonios under house arrest since 2006 for objecting to its meddling in church affairs, and has deposed him from his position as leader of his church.

The regime makes all other religious groups illegal. Imprisoned . . . evangelical and pentecostal Protestants routinely are tortured and pressed to recant their faith. . . .

Both USCIRF and the US State Department concur that Eritrea is one of the world's worst religious freedom environments, with the State Department designating Eritrea a "country of particular concern" or CPC each year since 2004.[4]

Yet the story you'll read in this chapter tells us that the brightest lights are shining even in the darkest places. For those of us living in safety, it seems we are willing to suffer so little to speak the name of Jesus. There was nothing in the world that would stop Adonay from speaking that name.

**ADONAY** || *Eritrea*

*Just twenty-seven years old, Adonay is a tall, thin, quiet, and humble man. It's his first time to talk to a Westerner. As he tells his story, he can still smell the sweat and urine of so many prisoners and guards. He can feel the pain of ropes tightening on his wrists and beatings too numerous to count. He can taste the dry bread thrown to him twice daily. His face is radiant with the love of Christ, but he speaks in a monotone, a note of despondence in every word. He recites the horrors as if he's relived them a dozen times, words like* almaz *rolling off his tongue as if he were discussing the weather.*

*Almaz is a method of torture favored by Eritrean jailers. Guards tie prisoners' elbows together behind their backs and then hang the prisoners from their elbows from the ceiling, a tree, or a post, just high enough for their feet to touch the floor on tiptoe. The victims' arms swell to the point of bursting, and the pain is so intense that they feel death is imminent.*

*Other methods are also common, such as "the helicopter." The victims lie face down. Their torturers tie their hands and feet together behind their backs, usually with a rope. Sometimes they are left on the ground in that position, often kicked and beaten. Many people we met stated this was how they were tortured. Others have said they are sometimes covered with sweet liquids to invite insects to bite their flesh, or hung from a tree or ceiling and left to swing for days on end, thus the name "helicopter."*

*Eritrean prisoners may dream to be released, yet if they do leave prison, they are either forced into the military or otherwise marked. They rarely can find work and often are reduced to begging. Christians in Eritrea know what to expect if they are arrested. Believers in prisons get the worst torture and the least food.*

*Even without torture, prisoners in Eritrea suffer extreme desert heat. The nation, a desert on the Horn of Africa just north of Ethiopia, is a "Country of Concern" for human rights violations. A United Kingdom diplomatic report states that "Eritrean prison conditions are life-threatening, harsh, degrading and unhygienic. Prisoners are subjected to physical and psychological torture, and cruel, inhuman and degrading treatment. Deaths from torture, overcrowding, disease, inadequate food and other harsh conditions are frequent."[5]*

*Enter fourteen-year-old Adonay. Just a boy, only two years in the faith, he was imprisoned because of his Christian beliefs, yet he held them steadfast for years while being tortured beyond imagination. Adonay even spoke boldly of Jesus to prison officials and dedicated himself to serving his fellow brothers and sisters in the prison, putting his life on the line to get them help from the outside world.*

*Adonay would be a remarkable person to meet under any circumstances. At the end of our conversation, he smiles for the first time, which lights up his face. His radiance is thrown into even greater relief by the degradation and evil he faced growing into adulthood in an underground prison.*

*His story is the longest in this book, but I ask you to read every single word. Read a paragraph again if your mind wanders. He deserves to have his story known, and I know that it will inspire and challenge you, as it has me.*

*There is a cost for some to follow Jesus. Adonay was only a teenager when he had to pay it.*

66 I came to Jesus at age twelve, when my friend invited me home with him. His parents led me to Jesus and had a big impact on me. But my parents were against me immediately. They were told that if I didn't renounce Jesus, they would be punished. I often heard, "We don't need you" or "Why don't you leave?" They put so much pressure on me. I lived that way for two years, until the day things got even worse.

When I was a teenager, our church had a wedding. One of my Christian brothers was marrying his wife. But government spies were in the church, so during the celebration, security forces came and took us all to jail. The soldiers said other churches were okay, but our church was not recognized by the government. Our church taught us to be born again.

So our entire church family started the journey of prison life. They took us to a mountain region called

"Forto." It was a former military camp and now an underground prison in the mountains. Then they separated me and took me to another prison because I was a kid.

At that prison, the guards would take me at night and question me. "Who brought you to the faith? Can you leave it? Can you leave Jesus?" When I wouldn't renounce my faith, they would beat me while everyone else was asleep. They tried to persuade me to leave Jesus. They said, "If you stop your Christianity, you can leave right now and return to school."

After twenty-seven days, they brought me back to the Forto prison. While I was gone, there had been a large roundup of Christian families in another city. Security forces went from house to house and collected Christians from homes and schools. They brought about sixty believers to the Forto prison. There were mothers with children, pregnant women, and older people in their sixties or eighties. Many of us were teenagers. They put us all together in a cell.

Early one morning, a military transport came, a large vehicle. The guards started calling us by name. When your name was called, you had to enter the transport. In our transport, we had forty people, thirteen women and twenty-seven men. We loaded into the transport and they started driving. It was still early in the morning, but we didn't follow the main roads. They didn't take us near the city. They took us around the city so we would not be seen.

We traveled northeast to a mountainous area and finally came to a military prison. It's mountainous, but it's still a lowland, a desert, so it's very hot there. The prison had criminals and many political prisoners. All the believers were in a very small area in the center. "Christians" were a special kind of prisoner. Other prisoners, even criminals, were considered to be faithful to the government. They had four-foot by four-foot cells and regular meals. Not us.

To be designated a Christian was not good. They gave us two pieces of bread twice a day and a tiny bowl of watery soup that was supposed to have lentils. It had no taste, no nutrition. That was all we would eat, day after day. The prison was very hot and dirty, but we were allowed to bathe only once a week. That meant we were hot and dirty all the time, plus we had bugs. People in our group would itch. If we scratched, it would cause a painful skin disease we call *hakakin*.

The head of the prison was a lieutenant colonel named Wedi Gile. After we were there a week, he collected the Christians and gave us a speech. He said our church was created by the US government and was financed by the United States. He talked for a long time. He said things like, "You may not know that, but your leaders know. You've been deceived by your leaders, so you better renounce your faith."

The guards were there with written statements for us to sign, saying that we agreed to deny our faith. For young people, if we would sign the statement, they said we could finish our education. This is where the separation came within our group. Few people remained faithful.

The lieutenant colonel asked one teenager, "Which side are you on? What is your community?" He said, "I am from the community of Jesus." It was a bold thing to say. The lieutenant colonel became very angry. He asked again, and the teenager would answer. The lieutenant colonel would say, "Don't make me angry," then he would groan. Finally, he said, "I will ask a last time, who is your community?" The teenager said, "I'm a Christian!" The lieutenant colonel slapped him. Then he yelled, "Take him away!"

The guards bound the teenager with a rope in a helicopter. They tortured him to make him an example to us. We were all afraid when we saw that. We didn't know what to say after that because we could see what could happen to us. He chose a girl. He said, "Stand up! Who is your community? What church do you belong to?" She came from a Pentecostal church. She was afraid, but still she admitted, "I am from Christian Life Centre." This gave us boldness.

The lieutenant colonel kept separating the group, based upon which fellowship they would identify with. After he divided us, the people who remained faithful numbered five women and eleven men. Two were under eighteen, but one was over sixty years old. In all, sixteen of us remained faithful.

The prison had a hierarchy. After you are there for a while, you may get some authority, respect, or responsibility, or even a nicer room. But none of us ever had that opportunity. We never had any privileges.

After a month, I got the *hakakin* skin disease all over

me—my hands, my private parts, my hair. I couldn't even hold the soupspoon. I couldn't wear trousers, so I had a piece of cloth over me. I couldn't urinate. I couldn't wash. I couldn't eat. I had terrible headaches. The other believers helped me with everything. For two weeks, the guards wouldn't give me any medication. Finally, they knew I was about to die, so they took me to a hospital. I received medication and slept there for a few days.

I was just a kid, so the prison officials decided it was the older believers that were keeping me from leaving the faith. They had the idea to separate me from the older ones, which meant to separate me from the other believers. So they took me to stay with the unbelievers. They thought maybe I would forget about my faith. Once I was pulled away, the guards alienated me, even at mealtimes. I couldn't have any comfort from my brothers. But I remained faithful.

A couple of jobs became common for believers within the prison. One was working in the laundry and another was tending to some woodland where we would chop and gather wood. After a while, I was allowed to work in the laundry. The laundry was right next to a large hospital, so I was able to move freely from where we stayed to the laundry and hospital. This gave us an opportunity.

Security wasn't very tight outside in the woodland, so some believers came from the nearby city and were able to bribe a guard to sneak things to us. In the prison, we received nothing, no hygiene products, just a little food. In the hospital, there were brothers imprisoned for other reasons, not their faith. The believers I was with would write a report for what each of us needed—hygiene products, food, even money. I served as the postman to pass our letters to the brothers in the hospital, and they would give them to the brothers from the nearby city, who would help us.

One time, I lost the paper! We were all so afraid, because our names were written next to our needs. The guards got the paper. They beat us and beat us. They beat us hard. Even the guards who had taken the bribes were punished because they had cooperated with us. After they beat us, from morning till night, they bound us in the helicopter and left us with no food for a day in the desert. For the guards who had taken bribes, they left them tied up in the wilderness even after they brought us back in.

That made us realize something was wrong. The government was frightened to think people from the outside world were contacting the prisoners. That would mean that people knew what was going on in the prison. It made us think we were in a secret prison to some degree and the officials wanted it to stay hidden.

Then one day, the guards decided to make me tend farmland. Just me. They would take me every day, all day, for about twelve hours. By evening, everybody was sleeping. So again, I didn't have much social interaction with believers anymore. It was like this for months.

Now, there was a toilet in the prison complex, but no one used it. They just went into the wilderness. The girls went a little further, and the guards didn't follow them. Some brothers from the nearby city would wait out there hiding and then would meet the girls to give them things for the believers. In the prison, we received nothing. But even after crackdowns, help was still coming from the outside.

When I started the farming job, I continued to deliver messages to the outside. Finally, officials realized that people in the wilderness were contacting the prisoners, so security got tighter. They started to follow the girls.

The farmland was near a village. One day, I saw a man who pretended to pass by me, but he said, "Do you know—?" and he named a girl. I was suspicious and ignored him, but then again he mentioned the girl's name, so I said, "Yes, she's my sister."

He had suspected I was a believer, so when I said "sister" to mean "fellow believer," he hugged me, and gave me some spiritual literature. But while we were talking, a soldier saw us. He said, "Adonay! Come!"

I always had notes and handwritten papers in my pockets, but I would hide them in the dirt in different places, scattered around the farmland. That way, if I were searched or questioned, I could go with empty pockets. On this day, the official demanded, "Where were you?" I had also thought of an alibi many days earlier, so I told him there was a shop nearby, and I was in the shop buying soap. "Here, look, here's the soap!" I said.

But he said, "We have information! Tell us the truth! You met a person and communicated with the girls!"

"I didn't go anywhere!" I said. "I didn't do anything! I just went to the shop!"

Regardless, they decided to teach me a lesson. It was another opportunity to try and break me and pressure me to leave my faith. I was tortured that day with the almaz method. In the prison, the toughest punishment was the almaz method. There is a tall wooden post, a brick underneath, and I had to stand on the brick. There was a rope hanging from the top of the post. They sometimes tied your elbows, but this time they tied my arms above my head with the rope around my hands. Then, they kicked the brick out from under me. All my body weight was hanging from my hands, but they made me touch the ground with the tip of my feet. I was shouting and shouting in pain.

"Tell us the truth!" they yelled.

"I did nothing!" I kept saying.

After they punished me, they took me to the lieutenant colonel. He said, "Tell me the truth! Don't do such stupid things. We caught you!"

They suspected a soldier was the person who was giving things to me, so they tied him up and brought him. They said to him, "Do you know this kid?" But both of us swore we didn't know each other. After that, they thought maybe they were wrong, so they started to believe me.

But then they started again on the usual topic. "Did you leave the faith?" And "You see, you are dying for this nonsense, just for the fellowship, the church!"

I said, "I am not in prison for the fellowship. I am in prison for Jesus!"

"You will die in here for your faith!" they shouted. "Your church is nonsense! You're imprisoned for this!"

Finally, the lieutenant colonel said, "Does the Bible say anything about these things?"

I said, "Yes! In the book of Matthew, chapter ten, it says, 'By my name you will be hated, and you will be put in front of officers.'" Just like that, those words of Jesus became true for him right then and there.

The lieutenant colonel mocked me. "Okay, I will see if your Jesus can save you," he said. "Take him and tie him up!"

So they tied me up in the helicopter. After they tied me for the whole day, they returned me to my cell.

Right after that, in an area almost seven hundred miles away, there was persecution. Officers brought believers from there all the way to our prison. We were all crowded in the same area together for months. Years had gone by, but I was still a teenager at this time. All this time, the other prisoners were free to go from here to there in the prison. But for us believers, they only opened the doors for us to get food and relieve ourselves.

When I was eighteen, they finally took some of us away from that prison. The believers who recently came remained there. But they took me and others to a place that was constructed by Italy back when Eritrea was a colony. The underground we were in was made for a water reserve, but it was turned into prison. Two rivers came down towards the prison, but there is no rain there. It is hot there, and no wind. You can light a candle outside and leave it, but it won't blow out. And it's a dangerous place.

Immediately, they told us that we could either renounce our faith and be in the military or be a prisoner. So there wasn't a real choice.

Before they took us into the underground, they took four of our group far away. They tied them in the helicopter. The ground was hot and rocky, and after they tied them, they left them on the ground and beat them. After they were beaten, three said, "Okay, we'll go." So the officials sent them to a military training location. Only one was left, because of a backbone injury, and went to the hospital.

After three days, we entered the underground prison. It was a terrible place. You would be disgusted to see it. There were some fellow believers there already. The officials insisted that we all had to renounce our faith and join the military. They would take us two by two and beat us each night. Five soldiers would beat one born-again Christian!

One by one, the brothers said, "Okay, we can't take it anymore." But they could not go home! There was no chance of freedom! They renounced their faith only to be sent to the military, which is much like a prison in our country.

I didn't have shoes when I went to this new prison. When there were newcomers, they would take us outside every afternoon and give us "military punishment," which was marching on the hot ground. It's hot like fire, and it's rocky. At first, my feet were swollen, so I limped as I walked. Then my feet were cut and bloody. Finally, my feet became hard and I could walk.

After a month of marching, we would think our punishment was finished. But each time new believers came to the prison, they would start this over again. Again and again and again.

By now, I was not afraid of the soldiers. They could tell I was stubborn in my faith. They didn't beat me first anymore because I was tough. They didn't want the others to be inspired by my strength. So they started to beat the others first as they demanded us to renounce our faith.

One day after beating me, they said, "We will beat you again." So they started beating me. But then they decided to beat the girls first. They started beating two sisters, Ayana and Rahwa, fellow believers. That day, Ayana died because of the beatings. After she died, the guards stopped beating us. But the next afternoon, they started the punishment all over again.

Later, the officials became afraid of the situation with the one sister dying, so they gave us work. They took me to be a farmer in the gardens. By that time, I had been there for months without shoes, and I worked in the gardens for [a] month in bare feet.

After almost a year in that prison, I had an opportunity to escape. I was able to flee to the nearby city, where I knew the believers would help me. I stayed there for over a year; then I was able to flee the country.

By the time I left prison, only two believers remained. The others had signed the statement to renounce their faith and had gone to the military. But one of the brothers who was in the prison with me has now escaped the country as well and is a Bible teacher. And he and I are both serving Jesus to this day.

✝

When we read Adonay's story, it's easy to be astonished at his faith and to think that he must be a super Christian to be able to stand firm when so many others had recanted their faith and when all human wisdom says "deny." The truly astonishing thing is that Adonay would tell you he is an "ordinary" believer, just like you or like me. He is not a super saint. He is as human as the rest of us are. He has simply been put in a situation where he has had to see the true power of his faith.

Nik Ripken (not his real name) has dedicated his life to demonstrating the love of Jesus in persecuted places and telling the stories of the bravery and faith of persecuted believers from around the world. In his book *The Insanity of God*, he recounts his meeting with a persecuted pastor in Russia. Overwhelmed by the stories he was hearing, Nik wondered why books and movies hadn't been made out of their heroic tales. The pastor's reply was as powerful as it was convicting:

"How many times have you awakened your sons before dawn and brought them to a window like this one, one that faces east, and said to them, 'Boys, watch carefully. This morning you're going to see the sun coming up in the east! It's going to happen in just a few more minutes. Get

ready now, boys.' How many times have you done that
with your sons?"

"Well," I chuckled, "I've never done that. If I ever did
that, my boys would think I was crazy. The sun *always*
comes up in the east. It happens every morning!" . . .

I didn't understand his point . . . until he continued:
"Nik, that's why we haven't made books and movies
out of these stories that you have been hearing. For
us, persecution is like the sun coming up in the east.
It happens all the time. It's the way things are. There is
nothing unusual or unexpected about it. Persecution for
our faith has always been—and probably always will be—
a normal part of life."

His words took my breath away.[6]

Nik's words took my breath away too—because this Russian
pastor's experience and the experience of persecution seems
worlds away from many of our lives.

I believe that, as followers of Christ, we have his Holy Spirit inside
us. It's my contention that if we were put in Adonay's situation or
in the situations Nik describes, maybe not all of us, but more of
us than we think would choose, as Adonay did, not to deny Jesus.
I think there is something about the power of Jesus in the life of
a Christian that causes us to rise to the occasion. If we really are
on a path of discipleship, if we really are saved, I think there's a
special grace for us in moments like Adonay faced to trust in Jesus
and remain committed to him.

And yet, let's be honest.

Many of us here in America *are* denying Jesus.

We're denying what we believe about Jesus when we don't tell other people about him. The question is, why are we denying him?

We will always have a lopsided Christianity if we are not exposed to the reality of suffering in the world. Our faith—for two thousand years—has never been complete without either being exposed ourselves to persecution or living in proximity to those who are persecuted.

So we struggle to be bold, because we've never known the power of God that rises up in believers only when they face suffering for their faith.

We will never experience full Christian discipleship if we aren't persecuted or if we aren't praying for, praying with, or living alongside those who are persecuted.

Ours is necessarily a suffering faith—Christ himself suffered, and we are to be like him—and it has been that way for two thousand years. And so without that part of the story—of our own stories—then our faith will be incomplete.

We must get closer to the persecuted church.

# CHAPTER 8

# I WILL NOT FEAR, FOR I KNOW HE IS ALWAYS WITH ME

*Even though I walk through the valley of the shadow of death, I*
*will fear no evil, for you are with me; your rod and your staff, they*
*comfort me. You prepare a table before me in the presence of my*
*enemies; you anoint my head with oil; my cup overflows.*

PSALM 23:4-5, ESV

**THE STORY YOU'LL READ** in this chapter is unique. Nearly every story I've heard firsthand or read that involves Boko Haram centers on their storming a Christian village, killing the males (older boys and men), and either leaving the women and children, or, more often, taking them into captivity and sexual slavery. For example, Reuters reported that "Cecilia Abel [a freed captive] said her husband and first son had been killed in her presence before the militia forced her and her remaining eight children into the forest."[1]

There are countless stories like Cecilia's where Boko Haram is concerned. While receiving very little media attention, the atrocities committed by Boko Haram are equal to those committed by

ISIS in Syria. The only difference is that Boko Haram has been at it much longer, and they've focused almost exclusively on Christians, whereas ISIS's bloodlust has been extended to all other religious communities in Iraq and Syria.

Our world lets Boko Haram continue its barbarity, and it's an embarrassing shame. But God's power over fear can be seen even in the midst of Boko Haram's terrifying acts.

## ISAAC || Nigeria

*Isaac walks down a busy street with a smile. He looks like your average thirtysomething, a regular guy—just a really happy one. Through the straps of his sandals, you can see the scars on his feet as he walks, unsteady and limping. He sits down and orders a coffee, excited to launch into his story. Soon you realize he is excited just to be alive.*

*A truck hitting him on his bicycle is how it all started. That's the accident that gave him the limp. A clinic treated him and then sent him to a hospital in the northeast for therapy. His problems really began there, as that is the home territory of Boko Haram. At Easter, the hospital released him to celebrate in a neighboring village, and it was on the way back from the celebration that both he and another believer were captured.*

*Few men survive the hate-fueled pogroms of Boko Haram, intent on exterminating Christians and imposing Sharia law. Non-Muslim women are sometimes captured. Non-Muslim men are exterminated. Yet the militants kept Isaac and his friend alive—for months. The two*

*were forced to see and hear the bloodthirsty Boko Haram militants
commit murders. For unknown reasons, none of the soldiers laid a
hand on either of them.*

*Isaac has yet to see his father since his escape. His mother died,
and now his siblings are scattered. Isaac is the youngest. Even
though he's not with his family, he is getting back on his feet. He
is in an apprenticeship program, doing well. He carries with him
the pay stub to prove it. Isaac is a free man, following his dream,
grateful to God, thankful for life.*

"After I had a serious accident, the hospital treated me and
transferred me to the north for therapy. I started to hear
about Boko Haram there, how they were killing, destroying villages, destroying properties. At the hospital, I saw
dead bodies leaving for the mortuaries because of Boko
Haram.

On Easter, I went to a nearby village to celebrate with
fellow churchgoers. After the celebrations, five friends and
I were traveling back. Before we got far, we came to a Boko
Haram roadblock. There was no way to escape. They saw
us before we saw them, and they had guns.

They picked on me because I was on crutches. They
said, "Drop to the ground!" Then they ordered me to follow
them into the bush, where there were many other members of Boko Haram hiding. As I walked from the vehicle,
my friends tried to run. One fell while running. A militant
put a gun to his head and tied his hands. My other friends
escaped into the bush.

Then Boko Haram stopped another vehicle with about

six members of the Canooli tribe inside. "Are you Muslim or Christian?" one of the gunmen said. They said they were Muslim. The extremists asked what village they came from, then demanded money "to do the work of Allah."

The leader asked me if I was a Christian or a Muslim, and I told him that I was a Christian. He said, "You are not a believer!" By "believer," they meant a Muslim. He said, "You are a disbeliever!" He said the men would slaughter me because I was a disbeliever.

The jihadists collected my money, things I had in my wallet, my ID cards. Then they collected the other men's things. They said they would release those who were Muslim, but they would slaughter anyone who wasn't. They said I would be killed. They ordered me to stand up again and follow them. We walked toward the main road, a gun at my head. I felt that the Spirit of God told me they would kill me, so I started praying right then. "God forgive my sins . . ."

One of the gunmen spun around and shouted, "What are you saying?" I said, "I am praying that God will forgive my sins." He said, "How do you know Allah?" I said, "I know God created you and me." They all laughed. The man said, "Does the disbeliever really know Allah?" Then he shot the gun three times to intimidate me, to show me it was a real gun.

"Get up," they said to the believer who was still on the ground. They directed both of us to enter our vehicle. They drove me and the man to another village in the bush, where they had their motorcycles. They started to interview each of us. They asked if I was a security man or a soldier. They discussed together about my leg injury. I said it was from a bicycle accident, but they insisted it was from war or combat of some sort.

Boko Haram put my Bible, my prayer books—everything I had brought with me—in a bag. They said they would burn it all. But later they gave me back some of my things. They said I should be writing books on Islam and some of their prophets, and if I did, they would return me to where I came from.

We heard the sound of gunfire, so the men put us back into the vehicle. I don't know what happened to the Canooli Muslims they stopped. Our car went on to another village. Boko Haram celebrated as they approached and said, "We have people to slaughter!" Me and my friend just prayed in our hearts.

Later, Boko Haram called some of their leaders who spoke better English. Those men questioned us. They thought maybe we had people or family that could send a ransom for us. But my friend said he had no one to give him any money. They asked if I had anyone who might put money forward for me. "I just came from the hospital," I said. "I am alone, without family. I don't have anybody to help me."

"There is no need for you to go back to the hospital," they said. "You will suffer there. You should stay with us. We can help you with your condition." So we stayed in that village for a few days, but of course they didn't care for us, except some food every now and then. In that village, they said they would release us. They made us study the Koran and read other books, but they said they wouldn't force us to change our religion.

After three days, I thought, *Nobody has killed us yet*, and I was encouraged. A few days later, we were traveling, and I saw we were near the village where we came from. I could sense Boko Haram thought we would try to escape, so they moved us to a different camp, very far from that village and in a thick forest. We had no idea where we were.

We stayed at that camp for a while; then they transferred us to another camp. We prayed very hard. We kept pleading with the militants to let us go. Since their leaders weren't there, they said they couldn't, but once the leaders were back, they said they could let us go. I knew this was a lie, of course. They transferred us to another camp, then took us back to the last one. By now we had spent months in captivity. We always asked them to let us go, but they said they couldn't without their leaders.

At one point, my friend worked up the courage to ask if he would ever see his family again. They said they would let him go, but they wouldn't let me go. Then they said that they would take me to the Sambisa Forest and I could choose from any of the kidnapped Chibok schoolgirls to be my wife!

Once again they promised they would release my friend, but time kept going by. The militants asked him if he had any way of contacting his wife. He said no. They said they wouldn't let him leave unless his wife could come meet him at the camp. Then we realized they weren't going to let either of us go, so we started to think about escaping.

By now it had been many months. Sometimes they brought food for us, and other times no food. We lived in a room fashioned under a tree, similar to a Fulani herdsman's home in the bush. It was hidden, so a plane couldn't easily spot us.

They brought others they had kidnapped. Some were Muslims, because we saw their documents. They interviewed them and saw that they were really Muslim. After a few days, those people said they wanted to go see their families, but instead our captors killed all of them in the bush. Many times people fake they are Muslim to protect themselves from the jihadists. Somehow the gunmen determined that they weren't "real Muslims."

After we saw that, we were afraid to ask to be let go anymore, because we thought maybe now they would kill us. So another two months passed, and we kept praying. It was not near the rainy season, but I thought, *If the rain falls, it will be easier to escape because they can't see our tracks to follow us.* But I was on crutches, of course, so we couldn't move fast. And if we escaped, we could easily stumble upon another Boko Haram trap and get captured again.

One day, they brought two more captives into the camp. They let one go, but they tied the other one's hands and legs. They claimed he knew security secrets about the Nigerian military and the police and demanded him to tell them. He was a civilian and a Muslim, but somehow Boko Haram was sure that he had knowledge of some important information. Then they called us out into the bush and forced us to watch them slaughter this man. They cut off his head.

We really started to fear after seeing this killing. Whatever they told us to do, we did it and stayed quiet. We feared for our lives every day. My friend decided we should pray and fast for three days. "Maybe God will touch their hearts," he said. After we fasted and prayed, their leaders still never came around, and we weren't released.

Many months went by. We still couldn't escape because there was too much security. So we waited. My friend was afraid to try to escape. Finally at the end of nine months, I said, "We don't know if one day they will just kill us! It is better that we just leave."

We prayed and fasted again, this time for five days. We prayed that God would bring rain. One afternoon, rain fell. It continued to rain all afternoon. That night we decided this was the day we would escape. We had some paper from tearing pages out of their books. We wrote our addresses, details about where we were from, who our families were. We put the paper in our pockets so that in case we were killed, we could be identified.

That night, the security fell asleep with their guns. I woke my friend and we went outside. We thought maybe they would see our footprints in the ground. So we walked for a while, then turned back and entered the bush a different way.

We kept moving into the bush. At daybreak, after all of our walking, we thought we had gone far away, but then we heard their morning prayer. We realized we had just walked all night in a circle! We were still near their camp. We hid in the forest right where we were. We slept for a bit. When we awoke, we saw snakes, but we weren't afraid. We thought maybe they would protect us, and we prayed for God to keep the snakes away from us. We forgot about the snakes and went back to sleep.

Night fell again, and we started to walk through the bush. We had no food. We drank rainwater. For three days, we didn't know where we were. We didn't want to enter any villages, because we knew Boko Haram was in the area and we didn't want to get caught again.

On the fourth day, we started getting very hungry. I was still injured, so it was tiring. We could often hear Fulani herdsmen in the distance, so I suggested we try and meet them, and maybe they would give us some food. My friend said no, we should just keep moving, in case the herdsmen would turn us in to Boko Haram.

Later that day, we saw a man near a village in the bush. He wanted to pass by on a bicycle. We had long beards from months of not shaving. He was afraid of us. But we decided to ask him anyway. He could not speak our language, so we motioned if he had food and water. He brought some food and water for us. We motioned to ask which road could reach the expressway to the larger city.

He pointed in one direction. He motioned it was very far, and we couldn't get there in one day. We start[ed] moving again on the fifth day.

One time, we spotted people near the main road. These

people saw us and noticed our long beards. They shouted to others, "Two Boko Harams are coming!" talking about *us*. We knew they went to inform security. But all they did was watch our movements, so we moved through there very fast. Finally, another man helped us reach the main expressway we were looking for. We came upon another town. We decided we should shave first so they wouldn't think we were Boko Haram. We found some equipment and cleaned ourselves up.

After that, we entered the village, and they gave us water. So we knew they thought we were *not* Boko Haram. We waited in the grass by the road, hoping to see some Nigerian security officials. We saw some enter the place where the people were who gave us water, so we went to them. As we approached, those people said they had seen us before. The soldiers and security officers all pulled out their guns. They all moved in a circle around us, thinking maybe we had other militants waiting in the grass.

When we reached their leader, he said they could put down their guns. We said we were with Boko Haram for a year. They gave us a change of clothes and let us clean our bodies. The officers checked our clothes, our pockets. They saw my hospital card, my baptism card, and my address that I wrote and put in my pocket. They even saw a note I wrote about being detained and about my long story. My friend also had written his story, too, and the captain read it all.

After the captain read everything, they took us to a hospital for treatment. They gave us some medicine and took care of us. A soldier gave me his phone to use. I called my brother. I said, "It's me—Isaac!" My brother said, "What?!" I said, "It's me—Isaac!" Then he hung up the phone because he did not believe I was still alive and he was scared.

They gave the soldier's number to my uncle. My uncle called, and again I said, "It's me—Isaac!" He said, "I want to speak with Isaac!" I said, "It *is* me; I'm Isaac." This time, he believed me. My friend reached his family, and they came for him. My uncle came and signed for me. I spent three days in my uncle's house. Many people came to greet me there. But soon security advised me to leave the area. So many people came, and one of them could be Boko Haram. It was better for me to leave.

The security took me to the hospital, and the doctors gave me another surgery. When I recovered, I was able to get trade training, and now I am an apprentice. I miss my family. But I am grateful to God for answering prayers and sparing my life. 🙶

Isaac's story is remarkable not just because Boko Haram kept him alive but also because of the courage Isaac displayed in their midst. When we believe in God, we are courageous. Courage is supernatural; it draws from the confidence we have in God because of the love God has for us. The Bible says, "There is no fear in love" (1 John 4:18).

Because Jesus loves us and because we love others, as Christians we remain courageous despite the trials and the troubles we might face in this world. God is powerful enough to be with us in the most difficult and challenging circumstances, and he reminds us that there's more to this world than what appears directly in front of us. Our "bodies are dying" but our "spirits are being renewed every day" (2 Corinthians 4:16, NLT).

I've prayed 2 Corinthians 4:18 in my life ten thousand times and with varying degrees of faith—and sometimes desperation: "We don't look at the troubles we can see now; rather, we fix our gaze on things that cannot be seen" (NLT).

Stories like Isaac's encourage and challenge us because they force us to ask the question, just what are we afraid of?

Are we afraid of what other people might think about us, or might say to us, or even might *do* to us? As a Christian, I recognize that the opposite of fear is faith. Jesus tells his disciples, "Don't be afraid of those who want to kill your body; they cannot touch your soul" (Matthew 10:28, NLT). There is a force stronger than our fear.

One of the first things to fall away when we are in a growing relationship with Jesus is our fear. It is at least difficult, if not impossible, for fear and faith to coexist. If we believe what the Bible says about Jesus, we understand that nothing can separate us from Christ's love.

The persecuted church proves to us that faith is stronger than fear. If they do not give in to fear when their faith faces such trials, then how is it that our fears bind us up so hopelessly?

The apostle Paul writes, "God has not given us a spirit of fear, but of power and of love and of a sound mind" (2 Timothy 1:7, NKJV).

We don't need to be afraid. God's Spirit is *powerful*—God gives us the strength we need when we act according to his will. And this power gives us the ability to love others, no matter the risk. God's Spirit compels us to care about other people, and because we care about them, sometimes we do things that are dangerous or sacrificial. But God's Spirit also gives us a *sound mind*, meaning that we aren't to take irrational risks. Rather, whatever risks we take are founded on the very real knowledge that God is working in us and for us, calling upon all of his power on our behalf. As Paul writes, "If God is for us, who can ever be against us?" (Romans 8:31, NLT).

Whether or not you face persecution, I am sure you know what it's like to face fears. May your fears always be subservient to the power of the love of Jesus. His love is stronger than your ultimate fear, even the fear of death.

# CHAPTER 9

# MY BATTLE IS NOT AGAINST FLESH

*Put on all of God's armor so that you will be able to stand*
*firm against all strategies of the devil. For we are not fighting*
*against flesh-and-blood enemies, but against evil rulers and*
*authorities of the unseen world, against mighty powers in this*
*dark world, and against evil spirits in the heavenly places.*

EPHESIANS 6:11-12, NLT

**IN CHINA,** the government-approved churches are part of the Three-Self Patriotic Movement, which is an arm of the Communist Party. Three things are important to note about this arrangement:

1. There are good individual churches in the Three-Self Movement.
2. There are good individual members in those churches.
3. The administration itself is often *antithetical* to Christianity.[1]

The house church has been and is the epicenter of the mighty movement of God in China. On and off again, house churches have moved progressively from the shadows and into the sunlight—and government concern.

At the present time, instances of persecution and arrest of Chinese Christians are clearly on the rise.[2] In 2014, one of the largest churches in China was demolished by the government, using the excuse of violations of "zoning regulations."[3]

As Gao describes in the story below, "There is black smoke on the land of China." He believes spiritual attack is actually what is behind the oppression and persecution by the Communists. Yet even while such spiritual attack persists, in China and elsewhere, Christians are called to remember that "our struggle is not against flesh and blood"—against other *people*—"but against the rulers, against the authorities, against the powers of this dark world and against the spiritual forces of evil in the heavenly realms" (Ephesians 6:12). We cannot hate those God has called us to love.

## GAO || *China*

*A stocky man with big, black hair steps off a bus and flashes a huge smile. He has a friendly demeanor and rushes to shake hands. He's a mover and shaker in the Chinese underground church movement and has the outgoing traits of a successful pastor—a natural "people person." But Pastor Gao is not the usual pastor.*

*In the last thirty years, Gao has been arrested forty-eight times. Yet he remains bold and courageous, unafraid and unapologetic in his faith. He has formed a legal defense network for house church pastors and has even written open letters to Chinese leaders, calling* them to do something about the persecution of Chinese Christians. He is a fighter. He works hard, too.

When he's not in prison, Gao bicycles from church to church, out in open streets, distributing literature and training leaders. Gao's focus is on Chinese young people. He has led thousands to Christ. Recently he has also focused his work on advocacy in the West, asking Western media outlets to pay attention once again to the serious persecution happening in China.

"I have friends outside China who help our ministry. I am not allowed outside of China, and they aren't allowed inside China, but we are friends! The government doesn't allow me to do certain things. We have restrictions on the amount of people that can come to our meetings—never more than thirty people. I can't receive foreigners, either. But we continue training leaders from all over China. Each leader we train has approximately one hundred churches under them, so the work in China is exponential.

We have a house church alliance to train leaders and also to help persecuted house churches, defending their freedom to worship. Anybody who joins the home church alliance is technically a criminal, according to the government. We have lawyers that are helping them.

I have been arrested forty-eight times, but I have never been convicted of a crime. My wife has been arrested thirty times. All of my personal phones are monitored, and I have five phone numbers. The government always tries to infiltrate my relationships. They spy on me and my colleagues and try to spread rumors. They have tried to lure me into saying bad things about others, but I refuse. They send spies to my congregation, but they can't really do anything. I recently changed the name of my organization so that the government can't trace my work as easily.

Thirty years ago, I became a Christian. I had a revelation from Psalm chapter 38. I noticed that after I accepted Christ, whenever I smoked, I would get sick, so I quit. Then four days later, as I was gambling, I got sick again. So I stopped gambling. From then on, I told everyone I met about Jesus.

At the time, there were legal accusations against me. I went to the "Upper Plea Bureau," which is a court of appeals for peasant people, but still I failed. That's when I realized there were no righteous officers in the government. There is black smoke on the land of China. It covers the whole sky. There is famine and disaster on our whole land. There is spiritual warfare in the CCP [Chinese Communist Party] that prevents us from living our lives.

I have been in trouble for thirty years, so I am now very experienced with how to handle the police. The first time I was arrested was because I was sharing Jesus during a sporting event. They put me in prison for 185 days. I fasted for 18 days, with handcuffs on my hands and shackles on my feet. After that, they found nothing wrong, closed my case, and released me, saying I was innocent.

That was very motivating and inspiring for me. I have since learned that my faith doesn't come from myself but from the presence of God. A year after that fast, I fasted for 41 days. Ten years later, I fasted and prayed for 120 days. Then

I made a road trip on my bike for four months, leaving with only six yuan in my pocket. A couple of years ago, I was in a serious car accident. Both legs were broken, but I recovered in only 23 days. This is all from the presence of God.

Two years ago, I went to Wenzhou to see where the government was tearing down Christian crosses. While there, I was arrested three times in three days. But each time, they couldn't charge me with any crime. After many hours, they would release me. Each time, the police would demand that I not have contact with "the outside world," with any Americans or any other foreigners.

The government is afraid now because of the growing numbers of Christians. I lived in Beijing for ten years, but the police banned me. Some believers have had very severe persecution. One sister was beaten to death in Guizhou province, in 2005. I helped her family to try to fight the government for financial compensation, but they were unsuccessful. Another sister in Shandong province was also beaten to death around that same year. This is uncommon now, though police policy and current national policy are supposed to protect against these killings.

During the Olympic Games of 2008, my wife and I were detained for twenty-five days and then placed on house arrest. At the same time, my son was beaten and seriously injured. They almost beat him blind. Years ago, I was also beaten quite seriously, but today, violence isn't as common.

As a Christian in China, God has given us the great mission to revive China's churches. In our organization, what we are doing right now is helping the religious people inside the church to become true believers—people with genuine faith. And that faith comes from the presence of God.

In the first years of a ministry called Promise Keepers, its founder, Coach Bill McCartney, rallied the men who filled stadiums with these inspiring words:

> God is saying to us: "Men, you've been in a war—but you have not been *at war*!" We've been retreating, but we're calling the men of God of this nation who live and stand beside the name of Jesus Christ to war. We have divine power to demolish strongholds, and we will contest anything that sets itself up against the knowledge of God! We will contest anything that sets itself up against the truth! We contest anything that sets itself up against Jesus Christ![4]

In the United States we can lose sight that ours is a spiritual battle. We live in a secular state, and the devil doesn't often use lavish displays of power here as he does elsewhere in the world. He doesn't need to—we're distracted enough from what God is doing. But if you go elsewhere in the world, and especially in places of severe persecution, it is obvious that there is more than meets the eye. There is a real spiritual war happening.

The evidence of this war is everywhere, not just in China—and it can sometimes seem like it's a war we've already *lost*. We are

JOHNNIE MOORE  ‖  109

now living at a time in history where Christianity has become the world's most persecuted religion and where Christophobia is a deadly reality in vast swaths of the world. The most conservative estimates suggest that it is now dangerous to be a Christian in at least sixty countries, and several of those countries are among the world's most populated.[5]

A report published in 2014 by Pew Research notes that in 2012 there were reports of government and social harassment against Christians in 110 countries—a much higher number.[6]

Christians suffer persecution from the most diverse group of regimes and religions:

- Atheist and Communist governments in China, Vietnam, and North Korea, to name a few
- Hindu fundamentalists in India
- Radical Buddhists in Sri Lanka
- Radical Muslims in the Middle East and Africa, which I wrote about extensively in my book *Defying ISIS: Preserving Christianity in the Place of Its Birth and in Your Own Backyard*

Of course, there are plenty of atheist leaders, Hindus, Buddhists, and Muslims who treat Christians with respect, but persecution is on the rise. Even in the United States, it has seemed at times like Christianity and Christians are on the defensive and sometimes in full retreat, or even that we've lost the war altogether. Christians are dismissed as bigots, and those who hold certain beliefs openly are chased from the public square. Even pastors write books and tell jokes about how bad the church is.

But I disagree with them. I believe the church is the best thing happening in the world. It is under physical and spiritual attack, but it's also on the march. And whenever the church is on the march, the enemy is eager to attack it.

It's par for the course. The light of the gospel has *always* come with the heat and smoke of persecution. The apostle Peter said it this way to believers under fire: "Dear friends, don't be surprised at the fiery trials you are going through, as if something strange were happening to you" (1 Peter 4:12, NLT).

But even in the midst of "fiery trials," don't lose sight of this: in every war there is an opportunity for victory. And I'm not talking of holy war or jihad. I'm not speaking of a crusade or of grabbing worldly weapons. I'm not speaking of a religious war but of a spiritual war. I'm talking about the power of the gospel, which needs no weapon to subdue hatred. I'm talking about the power that Jesus gives us to meet the bloodlust of terrorists or the corruption of Communists with the incapacitating power of perseverance and forgiveness.

These are the real miracles—the turn-the-other-cheek kind of miracles. There aren't enough bombs and bullets in the world to eradicate hatred, terrorism, and government-sanctioned persecution, imprisonment, and murder. The only thing that truly stops this hatred is the contagion of changed hearts.

And this is why it's important that, no matter where we are, no matter what situation we face, we remember that "our struggle is not against flesh and blood." The enemy would like nothing better than for us to keep our focus on our physical circumstances or on our enemies. But the apostle Paul describes the state of unbelievers like this: "The god of this age has blinded the minds of unbelievers, so that they cannot see the light of the gospel that displays the glory of Christ, who is the image of God" (2 Corinthians 4:4). And our situation was not much different before God saved *us*: "You were dead in your transgressions and sins, in which you used to live when you followed the ways of this world and of the ruler of the kingdom of the air, the spirit who is now at work in those who are disobedient" (Ephesians 2:1-2).

We recognize that just as those who persecute Christians now are blinded, we too were once enemies of Christ and were blind to our sin. Thus, "we do not wage war as the world does. The weapons we fight with are not the weapons of the world. On the contrary, they have divine power to demolish strongholds" (2 Corinthians 10:3-4). Our battle isn't against those who are spiritually blind; it is against the one who is blinding them, the devil.

And Scripture gives us a clear picture of how we wage war with the devil. In Ephesians 6, Paul writes about putting on "the full armor of God"—the belt of truth, the breastplate of righteousness, shoes "fitted with the readiness that comes from the gospel of peace" (verse 15), the shield of faith, and the sword of the Spirit (the Word of God). Most of these are pieces of defensive armor that allow us to stand when the devil attacks *us*, but the weapons we use are the Word of God and prayer. Paul writes, "Pray in the Spirit on all occasions with all kinds of prayers and requests. With this in mind, be alert and always keep on praying for all the Lord's people" (verse 18). Never underestimate the power of prayer and the Word of God. Sometimes, when I feel under personal attack—when I'm distracted or tempted or worried or disillusioned—I will use an app on my cell phone to read Scripture aloud. I can tell you that, without a single exception, the spoken Word has caused the attack to go away.

When Christians awaken to the plight of their persecuted brothers and sisters around the world, the question they ask is always "What can we do?" There are lots of things we can do—from speaking to our government representatives, to traveling to assist those in need, to giving financially, and so on—but one thing that all of us can do, and *must* do, is pray. We must "be alert"—we must *know* what our brothers and sisters in Christ are going through and care for them as we would our own physical family—and we must "always keep on praying for all the Lord's people." This may seem like a small contribution, or a passive contribution, but as followers of Jesus we believe that "the prayer of a righteous person is powerful and effective" (James 5:16). We believe this because *God* is powerful and is working on their behalf. But we must do our part.

When we recognize that our battle is not against flesh and blood, this realization, with the Holy Spirit's help, is what gives us the power to live out the next statement of the Martyr's Oath—"I will not hate those whom God has called me to love."

It is also what gives us the miraculous ability to forgive those who sin against us, as we will study in the next chapter.

# CHAPTER 10

# I WILL FORGIVE

*Forgive, and you will be forgiven.*

LUKE 6:37

**DESPITE ALL THE ATTEMPTS** through history to malign Jesus' teaching, at its very core, Christianity is Jesus' message of love to all people—love that is displayed in joyful lives and that perseveres even in brutal death. Again and again, those faced with the choice to "convert or die" in Syria, Libya, Nigeria, and elsewhere refuse to convert. Then they take advantage of their final, dying breaths to speak forgiveness to the faces of their murderers.

Forgiving their enemies is something these courageous men and women learned from the words Jesus delivered on a Roman cross—a device of final persecution and martyrdom. He used one of his own last breaths to say, "Father, forgive them, for they don't know what they are doing" (Luke 23:34, NLT). His words are a model for our response when we are maligned, insulted, threatened, or injured for Jesus, as we see in the stories of Sandy and Daniel.

## SANDY || China

*Sandy's maternal grandparents—and later her parents—were martyred for their faith. Her mother had led Sandy's father to Christ and then married him. Sandy's father was from a family of devout Communists. When her parents launched into ministry, her paternal grandfather was enraged. As a member of the Communist government, he had the power to have his own son arrested.*

*Other government employees took advantage of the fact his son was a Christian and turned it into a political nightmare for him. Eventually Sandy's father was killed in prison before her birth.*

*The Communist grandfather then tracked down her mother and killed her, too. So, just like her mother, Sandy became an orphan at a young age due to her own parents being martyred.*

*Sandy is quiet and shy. She still cries when she recounts the story of her parents. It's no wonder. She lived in hunger and poverty as an orphan in the homes of people who mistreated her. Although she was a gifted student, she was bullied in the university due to her youth and poverty. By God's grace, she has found the unconditional love she never received as a child.*

66 I am a third-generation Christian. When my mother was a teenager, her parents were martyred in the revolution. They were living in a small village when they were

arrested. They had their house properties and handwritten Scriptures taken. Then they were killed. So my mother was an orphan when she was young, but my mother stood strong in her faith in Christ.

My father didn't believe in Jesus when he met my mother. His family came from a military background. His father was a loyal Communist Party member. He fought in the army. But my father had a fascination with literature. My mother gave him a Bible to read. When he first started to read it, his heart was immediately drawn to it. He was inspired by the stories of Jesus, and he wanted to believe in him. My father converted to Christ.

His father was in a high government office. Other peer officers were jealous of my grandfather's position. It was impossible for my grandparents to support my father's faith. My father was the oldest but had two brothers. He had to split with his family because of his faith. My grand-father couldn't accept the fact that my father disobeyed, so he imprisoned his own son. My mother was pregnant with me at the time.

The incident was taken advantage of by the other peer officers. My father's case became a political issue. The case got out of my grandfather's control. Soon my grand-father regretted imprisoning his son, but he didn't have the power to release him. He would have to go to his peers to get their approval. Government officials organized a committee to interrogate my father, to persuade him to leave my mother and renounce his faith. But my father was killed in prison, simply because of his faith.

Even though my father had just died, my grandfather still tried to convince my mother to divorce him and have an abortion. Abortions were common because of the one-child policy. And girls were not wanted. But my mother felt the call to be a missionary, to go to other cities to plant churches. She left and went to a small county in Anhui province and gave birth to me there.

One month after she gave birth, she entrusted me to a woman in her village. She felt she had to leave me for my own safety and protection. She had a clear purpose for missions.

While my mother was gone, my grandfather sent the military to the town to look for my mother. My mother knew that her husband was killed, but the officials that came to get her lied and said to tell my mom that her husband was still alive. Somehow they found my mother. She was killed for her faith in Christ, just as my father was.

My life became rough. I was raised by an older couple. They didn't allow me to live in the main area of the house. I had to sleep out in the kitchen with their dog. I ate very little and was often very cold. I suffered from hunger all the time. At 4:00 or 5:00 p.m., I would see smoke coming from the chimney of the home I lived in. I would stand nearby, but I usually wouldn't get fed, because the family I lived with had a lot of kids. I would often go next door and maybe get lucky and others there would feed me.

I went to primary school. Because I was intelligent, one year I jumped three grades at once. I dreamed of opening a factory to produce food, because I was inspired by growing up in poverty. I went to college when I was fourteen years old. Other smart students came from wealth, but of course I came with virtually nothing. When it rained, I didn't even have rain boots. I had to put bags on my feet. I was also part of an institute at my university for gifted kids, but I didn't enjoy it there.

Eventually I moved to a different university. When I got there, I was often bullied because I was short, poor, and could usually only afford bread to eat. They would ruin my bread to bully me, so I began to get angry at God. Bitterness took hold in my heart. My foster family continually failed to take care of me well.

When I grew up, I went to visit some people at my mother's house church. It was torn down, but small cell groups were still meeting, all because of the commitment of my mother's evangelization to that community. Only older members are left of that congregation. I know that my mother must have suffered a lot. Some of the members of her congregation know what happened to my mother. Others don't.

My grandfather remained very stubborn. He still didn't accept what he did. He visited me in 2010 and told me that my faith is just superstition.

Later, at a house church, I met Anna. When we met, Anna showed me love and compassion. I experienced healing from being with her. I had low self-esteem, but I know I am called by God to ministry.

At first, Anna didn't want to try to be my mother. But two years ago, she allowed me to call her "mom." When

I did, Anna started to cry. A few months later, Anna read in Psalms that God would give the homeless a home, so she offered me a home with her and her husband.

Now my grandparents have passed away. But I still have to forgive them for being responsible for the ultimate killing of my father. In my church, people often say it's an honor that my parents are martyrs, but I deal with shame from it. I wish I could be a normal kid. It's still painful. Sometimes when I share these stories, I still sense bitterness rising in my heart.

But the greatest healing power is love. I've been living with Anna for one year now, and I know Anna will continue to show me more and more love. And most importantly, we are coworkers for Jesus. 🙶

**DANIEL** ‖ *Nigeria*

*A tall, thin African man hops his way into the hotel lobby and positions himself on a chair, then leans his crutches against a wall. Beneath his pants legs, you can see only one foot. The other leg is completely gone. Daniel is middle aged. Prematurely gray hair frames a face with a sober expression yet without a trace of worry or bitterness. When he speaks of atrocities, he speaks factually, without emotion. But when he speaks of Jesus, his voice warms; his face brightens. You can well imagine him as a man given to hospitality to those around him, loving others as he himself has been enveloped by the love of God.*

*His story is shocking. He has seen terrorists, Boko Haram, extremists. But he claims it was none of them who opened fire on him and his family. It was instead those the government had entrusted with protecting people like Daniel—the military sworn to uphold the law of the land. Controversy surrounds such stories. The fact that there are so many is what makes them believable. Daniel isn't the only one who claims "friendly fire." He's just the one with the missing leg, the murdered brothers, the paralyzed father, and the memories of horror.*

I had a truck and worked in construction. My wife and I have four children. Two will enter university soon. Our business was beside a main road. There was a Nigerian military checkpoint set up near our garage, a roadblock. My wife cooked for these soldiers every day. One day, one of the Muslim soldiers said he was given instructions to kill me. His bosses said we were fighting with the Muslim herds-men. But the soldiers told the other officers, "We haven't seen this. We haven't seen these people bothering anyone."

Two weeks later, there was an attack. They came on a Tuesday morning. We heard the sound of gunfire behind our business. So we decided to investigate and see what was happening. As we stepped out, there were people in front of me, and we heard gunshots getting closer. We thought it was Boko Haram.

They took their guns and opened fire on us. Two people in front of me fell to the ground. And then I was shot in the leg. I tried to hide in a garage nearby, but they found me. And they shot me again, this time in the thigh.

Then I recognized their uniforms. They were soldiers, not Boko Haram!

The soldiers left us and then started shooting people in nearby homes. They shot dead a woman in her home. They shot another woman with a baby on her back. The baby was killed. They don't spare our children, because they want to kill off the next generation of Christians.

Then a military convoy came with a machine gun truck. They picked up the soldiers and left. People in town came and took many of us to the hospital to be treated. Five people were buried that day, including two of my own brothers. My father is in a wheelchair now, paralyzed.

Someone asked me, "What would you do if you saw the soldiers who hurt you?" And I said, "Jesus says if you don't forgive, you won't be forgiven. So I have already forgiven them."

Forgiveness is a miracle—there's no other way to say it. It is a genuine miracle when Sandy, who doesn't remember her parents, can forgive her grandparents for their involvement in her parents' murders. It is a legitimate miracle when Daniel, disabled from wounds suffered from those who should have been protecting him, forgives those responsible for his current pain. Forgiveness is a miracle grander than the parting of the Red Sea or the feeding of the five thousand. It's also been the hallmark of our faith for two thousand years.

Yet God's call for us to forgive those who sin against us does not mean that God takes a passive approach to sin and evil. He's been fighting the effects of sin in our lives and in our world from the very beginning. The things that are bad and broken about our world are not God's fault—they're our fault, our sin.

*We're* the ones who have chosen again and again to harm one another. We're the ones who have started all the wars on earth. We've created the weapons that destroy us. We've created the economic systems that bind the poor. We've allowed tyranny and self-interest to pollute our politics so that the innocent are persecuted, manipulated, disenfranchised, robbed, and—in some places—imprisoned or even killed. We have created the need for countless instances of forgiveness, and God has changed our hearts so that we are capable of forgiving.

This is especially true when you consider Christian persecution around the world. Persecution may be sin's most personal attack against God's plan to love and to bless the world. Persecution is a sin that seeks out and has its way with vulnerable Christians in countries where they are not protected by religious freedom. It does this with a brutality rarely matched by any evil force at any point in history. The streets of the world run red with the blood of Christians. Sin's lust is never satisfied until it has feasted on just one more.

But with every final act of hate, perpetrators often hear a sermon that will haunt them for the rest of their lives: "I forgive you."

Christians around the world go through countless forms of suffering, yet God calls them to forgive their enemies. And they do it! What are our excuses for refusing to forgive ours? This issue of forgiveness speaks to the heart of the subtitle of this book: "living for the Jesus they're willing to die for." It is also at the heart of the gospel. Jesus, immediately after teaching his disciples to pray, offers additional commentary on just one of the phrases of the Lord's Prayer: "If you forgive other people when they sin against you, your heavenly Father will also forgive you. But if you do not forgive others their sins, your Father will not forgive your sins" (Matthew 6:14-15).

As people who have been forgiven by God, we *must* forgive others. We have no other option.

Our ability to forgive others might say more about the actual commitment we have to Jesus than anything else. If we cannot forgive, then we do not fully know the love and forgiveness of Jesus (see Luke 7:36-50). If we refuse to forgive, then we are refusing our faith. If forgiveness is at the heart of the gospel, then how can we profess to have been saved by the power of God in the gospel if we refuse to forgive?

These are not easy questions, but this is not an easy world. The stakes are far too high not to ask them. Whom must you forgive today?

Forgiveness is not a feeling; it is a choice. We must *choose* to forgive. In fact, choosing to forgive may not feel much like forgiveness at first, and it may take time. But when we announce that we forgive someone else, the Holy Spirit will give us the ability to fully and truly forgive. And it is this power that can and has changed the world.

# CHAPTER 11

# I WILL CLOTHE MYSELF WITH MEEKNESS

*A bruised reed he will not break, and a smoldering wick he will not snuff out. In faithfulness he will bring forth justice.*

ISAIAH 42:3

**ONE OF THE MISCONCEPTIONS** that I think many people have about the persecuted church is that it is weak and powerless. Certainly the propaganda from persecutors like ISIS would have us believe this—that militant extremism is on the march and weak Christians who get in the way will be mowed down on the way to a worldwide caliphate.

The reality, however, is quite the opposite. As the church father Tertullian said so long ago, "The blood of the martyrs is the seed of the church." In other words, there is nothing that can be done against Christians to stop our faith from growing.

Persecution is causing:

- The faith to grow as Christians demonstrate the love of Jesus.
- The faithful to grow as persecution proves and deepens the faith of true believers.
- The church to become stronger as casual Christians fall away, leaving only those who are committed to Christ.

As a Protestant reformer once said, "The church is an anvil which has worn out many a hammer." No prison can contain our witness. No censorship can contain our love. No hatred can contain our forgiveness.

How exactly does it happen that Christians get stronger when we are persecuted? One way is that the watching world sees the power of our God evidenced by the strength of our faith. They are at once appalled by the actions of our persecutors and amazed by our response. And they recognize that the power to stand firm isn't our own. Paul writes that "we now have this light shining in our hearts, but we ourselves are like fragile clay jars containing this great treasure. This makes it clear that our great power is from God, not from ourselves" (2 Corinthians 4:7, NLT). Resistance to the gospel melts away as we demonstrate love to our persecutors, pray for them, and return blessing for cursing (see Matthew 5:43-47; 1 Peter 3:9).

The virtue undergirding all this is meekness—which is exemplified in Mebrahtu's story.

## MEBRAHTU || *Eritrea*

*"We continued worshiping because if you don't have that, you don't have life," Mebrahtu said as he told his story.*

*Mebrahtu is vibrant and has an eagerness to be part of the team, to be one of the people who will change the world. It's hard to believe what he's been through—persecution, imprisonment, torture, strangulation, and escape. Yet Mebrahtu exudes a "hunger and thirst for righteousness" (Matthew 5:6).*

*In a hotel coffee shop, he sits and watches as one person after another recounts their stories. When he finally tells his, he is earnest, humble, and exceptionally intelligent. He is dead serious about his faith and has the story to prove it.*

" I became a born-again believer and was part of the Salvation Church of Eritrea. At that time there was no persecution from government, just persecution from the public. The society was calling us liars and deceivers.

The next year, problems came for the church, too. First, the government took our church. They closed everything. They forced us not to worship. Soldiers confiscated our church materials, Bibles, furniture—everything. They also took the church's money. Later, they came after us as individuals.

The Eritrean government told everyone, "This church is founded by America." They spread propaganda about their hatred of the West, America, and Christianity. The government is paranoid of any non-Communist influence and of any sort of religion or cultural structure they can't control. They don't like the American government. It's a scapegoat for them.

Our problem was first that the society didn't approve of us, so they were delighted when the government cracked down on us. Some traditional Christians were very against us. Secondly, the government hated us. We were in the middle of two fronts—the Communist government and the society.

From then on, we were forced to meet in home cell groups of maybe three to six people, because we had the desire to worship God, regardless of the situation. First, we had to find a Christian family to worship with. Then we had to be very careful. We would change the dates. Maybe we met on Wednesdays, then we changed to meet on another day. They were spying on us. We couldn't always hide, so sometimes they arrested us.

When they arrested us at first, they would just tell us not to do that, and they would let us go because we were youngsters. Later, they started demanding that we change our faith. If we did, they would let us go. But we couldn't say we did not worship God, so we couldn't sign the paper they gave us. It was very hard for us. Yet the Word of God says we have to trust the Lord, even in the hard times.

The first time the government approached me was when I was in high school, just a kid. I remember I was with an elder-in-training in the church. We were having some underground worship to God, and they found us.

We told them we wouldn't do this anymore, but we still did in other places.

Eritrea has forced military service. Everyone has to finish school up to eleventh grade, but if you want to continue after that, you have to go to military camp. So I went. If I wanted an education, I didn't have an option. In the military, you had to be very careful. You couldn't even say, "God bless you." We were very, very careful. We continued worshiping because if you don't have that, you don't have life.

The military camp was in a desert, with hangars and warehouse buildings but no hiding place. When we wanted to relieve ourselves, we would have to go in the wilderness, pair by pair. So the Christians would pair up so we could pray with each other. We would discuss our faith, write down a Scripture, and distribute it. Some of us had a Bible, but we had to hide it. For discussions, the Scriptures were only in our heads and our hearts.

We were very careful in how we did things, but we knew we wouldn't be able to hide forever. There are spies, and they know everything. One day the camp officials caught us. Even before they caught us, they knew I was a believer. They took me and tied my arms and legs behind my back in the helicopter method. Everyone gets that. It is very common.

Then, at 7:00 p.m., you normally get your dinner and go to sleep. But I was left alone outside; then they sent someone outside to strangle me. There was a sandstorm, like in the *Mission Impossible* movie. The person who was strangling me left. Even he went to sleep. I was just left alone out in the wilderness. There were hyenas and other animals around. Then I started to lose hope. The storm was very hard for me. It was midnight. I started crying, and I was praying.

I saw a land cruiser nearby, but it was totally dark. They couldn't see me. The car started to go in reverse and was coming toward me. I shouted, but I was still strangled and the storm was blowing. They had their doors shut because of the sand, and they didn't hear me.

A colonel happened to see me from the side. He ran and shouted, "Stop! Stop! Stop!" There were good people among them. They are not all devils. It was from God. They woke up the guy who tied me up and said, "Why did you leave him?" And he said, "Because he's a Pente." This is what they call a Pentecostal. So they said okay and let him go back to sleep.

That night was disastrous for me. Very hard for me. That was the first time something like that happened to me. Sometimes when hardships come more and more, you just don't care. So we started singing, and we just kept singing. So they came and brought us to a "maximum security" [shipping] container, a terrible place. The temperature in there would get very high. They left ten of us there for a week.

When we weren't in prison, we would take military classes, but they often punished us with sticks. They put us in the helicopter. It was just routine.

We were doing as the Word of God ordered us, to do

every single duty the military ordered us to do, but still they imprisoned us. We did all our government homework, yet they still imprisoned us. We started to lose hope.

When we went to prison, we saw people who were in there for many years. Most of them were innocent. There were Jehovah's Witnesses who were held for as much as ten years because they didn't do their duty to the government. But there were also some people that did some terrible things to the government too.

There was so much hardship. They were demanding we sign papers saying we would give up our faith. They would put us in the container all day. We could leave only to relieve ourselves. Then we ended up being left in there for almost three months. For me, it felt like three years.

I came for education, but instead I got this. My life plan was damaged. I came to the military camp to do the right thing, but I got this. After so much pain, they took us from that prison back to the camp. But because we didn't finish our military courses, we had to wait for the next round. It would take us one year to wait.

Then they gave us work to do. Really, it was like slavery. We were the slaves of the government. We were on a very large farm with vegetables. We harvested the vegetables for one year, and then we could go back to the classes and finish.

One time, they were celebrating Eritrea's independence day. They forced everybody to go. In the middle of it, there was a clash between a student and a policeman. They should have punished the one student, but they thought what he was doing was against the government. So they took us all back when the program ended at almost midnight. A few hours later, they woke up all the students. They took us outside, and we were just walking and walking. We had a routine of gathering wood once a week, so we thought that's where we were going. But we passed the wood area. Then we thought maybe we were going to collect stones. But we passed the stone area. It was total darkness, and we just kept walking. Finally, at dawn, we reached a very wide-open area. There were mountains but then nothing, not even a tree. The sun rose early, so it was light by then.

Then the leader of the battalion told us we were about to endure punishment for what happened last night. He said, "You have to go run in the mountain area five times! If you say anything, there will be consequences."

Every two meters there was a soldier watching us. We were so tired, but we had to run. The soldiers watched us and yelled at us in hatred. Running down the mountain, it was easy to fall. Some people fell and broke their legs! Everyone was distraught. I ran and ran. But there was no food and no water, so I fainted. A friend carried me until I could run again. We could not stop. The soldiers were ready to shoot. We could not escape.

When we finished our punishment, the injured students needed to be carried back. We saw government pickups and cars there, so we hoped they would take us. Instead, the soldiers said, "You need to carry them back!" So they forced us to carry the injured back. We got back at twenty-four hours after we had left.

We went to our beds exhausted. But they came and knocked on the doors and said, "Come out! You have another punishment." This one was called "Tsinae." You have to stand straight in the sun, no movement, for two and a half hours. People started to fall down. People fainted. I fainted. We couldn't tolerate it.

Even though I asked for forgiveness, I started to get angry at God. People in the camp were fleeing to Sudan. At first we had one hundred twenty in one regiment, but soon only eighty remained. Forty were able to flee. Some people were caught, and they made them an example to us.

I didn't want to go to another country. I wanted to finish my education, even with these complexities. Finally, I finished the military training; then I finished my education. At the end, you're given two weeks to study. If you pass the exams, you can join college. If you don't pass, you join the military. I passed.

I attended a technical school, but once again, because of my Christianity, there was persecution. I was alienated. One day the leaders strangled me for reading the Bible, but the next day they let me go. I didn't have to go to prison.

I was at school for four months. I was able to attend a technical school, but I couldn't pray or worship as I liked. When Independence Day came around, as usual there were many festivities. There were fundamentalist Muslims and devout Christians, and we said we couldn't participate in the carnival. For the Muslims, they let them go. They didn't force them to participate in the carnival. But for two hundred Christian students, they put us all in prison. We were there for almost two months. We tried to plead our case with them, but they wanted us to sign papers. Some of the students were new Christians, and eventually they signed the paper. For those of us who did not sign the paper, they took us to prison. We were in prison for close to a year.

At that time, a soldier I knew was able to negotiate with the government to get me out. I know God put him in that position for me. At the time, he wasn't even a believer, but he is now!

In my second year in school, I was very careful. I changed and went to a different school. I thought things would finally start to improve for me. But at the new school, the government would take students and brainwash them. Then they would train them to spy on us.

At first, we were free. Some groups like the Evangelical Lutheran Church and the Coptic Church were even recognized by the government. But they didn't recognize the Pentecostal Church. Then things became hard for us. They watched us. We couldn't freely worship God, and we couldn't even do the two-by-two program pairing off like we used to. But the government was afraid that the large churches would put pressure on them and tell the world what the government was up to. So they held back a little.

For me, I could read my Bible in my home, thanks to God. Especially when they were asleep. I would just say I was studying.

I finished school, but I majored in marine biology, so I had to take another test to be qualified to teach. The government wanted me to be a teacher, so they took me near the border. When I got there, I was able to flee. It was hard, but I was so grateful.

Most of the students I graduated with have also left Eritrea. My family has all come to Jesus. And now I am ready to worship God and to lead others to him. It is my desire and my joy.

The old saying that "meekness is not weakness" is exactly right, especially in the lives of persecuted believers like Mebrahtu. Far from being weak and passive, by meeting their persecutors with meekness and kindness, our persecuted brothers and sisters are actively sowing love in the midst of hate. We're not used to seeing real meekness and kindness, so it's easy to mistake it when we do.

But don't be fooled. Just because someone *can* claim their rights doesn't mean they have to. Just because there might be a way out of a situation doesn't mean that the strong thing to do is to escape the fight. Sometimes the strong thing to do is to remain, to turn the other cheek, to *endure*, because in taking the blows, that person might save the lives of others. Meekness is supernatural. It's strength under control. And while the persecutors want to appear strong, in actuality they're the weak ones. Our suffering brothers and sisters are, by their testimony, the strong ones triumphing over their persecutors' hate.

Meekness is necessary for followers of Christ. In the Beatitudes

Jesus tells his disciples, "Blessed are the meek, for they will inherit the earth" (Matthew 5:5). And Jesus' own example to us is one of meekness:

> Have the same mindset as Christ Jesus:
>
> Who, being in very nature God,
>> did not consider equality with God something to be used
>>> to his own advantage;
> rather, he made himself nothing
>> by taking the very nature of a servant,
>> being made in human likeness.
> And being found in appearance as a man,
>> he humbled himself
>> by becoming obedient to death—even death on a cross!
>
> PHILIPPIANS 2:5-8

Jesus' meekness is our salvation, and we are to follow his example. As we see in Mebrahtu's story, this might look like submitting to the governing authorities for the sake of Christ (see Romans 13). Or it might mean resisting government pressure to convert or to participate in activities contrary to Christian teaching, while in the process letting "your gentleness be evident to all" (Philippians 4:5).

It can be difficult for us, in a society that worships strength and fame and celebrity, to clothe ourselves in meekness, but that is what we are called to do. If meekness is "strength under control," how can we exhibit that in our culture the way our persecuted brothers and sisters are doing in theirs?

For many of us, this will involve surrendering our need to win or to have the last word. The reason we Christians can clothe ourselves in meekness in the first place is because of the certainty we have in Jesus that our sin debt has been paid. Our relationship with Jesus makes the rest of our life secure.

We say with the psalmist, "The LORD is for me, so I will have no fear. What can mere people do to me?" (Psalm 118:6, NLT). If we really believe that the Bible is true, it isn't necessary for the culture or the government to validate it. Yes, there are and always will be times when standing up for the truth is necessary. But there are also times when, in meekness, we leave room for the Holy Spirit to do his work. Our ultimate mission is not to win a cultural war; our mission is to present souls reconciled to God.

Further, meekness involves taking the servant's place and placing others above ourselves. On the night before his death, Jesus told his disciples, "Who is more important, the one who sits at the table or the one who serves? The one who sits at the table, of course. But not here! For I am among you as one who serves" (Luke 22:27, NLT).

When we truly clothe ourselves in meekness, our main goal is no longer self-preservation. Rather, our goal is to make Jesus known through our example. And because meekness seems rarer and rarer these days, at least in the United States, it has the potential to amplify our witness all the more.

# CHAPTER 12

# MAY THOSE AROUND ME SEE THE FACE OF JESUS REFLECTED IN ME

*You must worship Christ as Lord of your life. And if someone asks about your hope as a believer, always be ready to explain it. But do this in a gentle and respectful way. Keep your conscience clear. Then if people speak against you, they will be ashamed when they see what a good life you live because you belong to Christ.*

1 PETER 3:15-16, NLT

**ONE OF THE MOST AMAZING PROMISES** in Scripture is one you no doubt know by heart: "We know that God causes everything to work together for the good of those who love God and are called according to his purpose for them" (Romans 8:28, NLT). In other words, God can use any situation for our good and his glory. Any situation—even the most unlikely.

As it relates to persecution against Christianity, and particularly persecution at the hands of extremist Muslims, it's easy to construct a terrifying narrative:

- Extremist Muslims are slaughtering, imprisoning, and torturing Christians with impunity in their lands.

- In the context of this "religious cleansing," the Middle East is being emptied of Christians.
- The civil war in Syria and the war with ISIS in Syria and Iraq has resulted in a mass exodus of potential terrorists to the West.
- They are growing stronger; we are growing weaker.
- Muslims are poised to become the majority, especially in Europe—if only by virtue of their higher birthrates.

While there is an element of truth to these things, it is vital to recognize that these events present an unprecedented opportunity for the cause of Jesus. *Right now* the Holy Spirit is moving in powerful ways in this part of the world, drawing people to himself and getting them in a position to freely choose him. The result: a jaw-dropping exodus from the crescent to the cross. And because of what I'm about to share, it is vital for you to look at the events of the day *in a completely different way.*

In the appalling brutality of persecution, it's easy to lose track of the simple truth of John 3:16—God loves the world and sent his Son to save it. God has not written off Muslims or the Muslim world. In fact, he loves them dearly, and he's reaching out to them in supernatural ways, through dreams and visions. One woman from a Muslim background told CBN News, "In the church if you ask how many people came to Jesus, 80 percent will say, 'I saw Him in a dream.'"[1]

Missionary-turned-researcher David Garrison says, "We are living in the midst of the greatest turning of Muslims to Christ in history."[2]

Because of the intense persecution of those who abandon Islam for the gospel, this awakening is not readily *visible*, but it is *real*.

There is no doubt that the civil war in Syria is a humanitarian catastrophe—the worst in our time—nor is there any doubt that worldwide strife and mayhem caused by the likes of ISIS constitute an unmitigated evil. Nor is there any doubt that the Spirit of God is working in the midst of all this to draw displaced people to himself.

In this chapter you will read the stories of Mani and Aliya. Mani, despite receiving many offers to relocate, has remained in Syria to minister to the Muslims there, though he and his family face great risks. Aliya's story illustrates how magnetic the love of Jesus is to our Muslim neighbors. Both stories show us the importance of reflecting the character of Jesus to those around us.

## MANI || *Syria*

*Caught in the clash between politics and religion, Pastor Mani, his wife, and their two sons have made the brave decision to be a bright light in a very dark world. Mani is of average height, with curly hair and a stocky build. He explains, "Yes, there is destruction and many problems. But on the other side, you see many turning to God and coming to know Jesus."*

*If the key to real-estate investment is "location, location, location," the last place a responsible parent would plant a young family is in Syria. But if your goal is to make an eternal investment in the Kingdom, this is the area of the world where the harvest is plentiful and the workers are few, and every worker is critical.*

*Pastors, Sunday school teachers, church workers, and*

*congregation members are still fleeing Syria. Back in 2015, the* New York Times *was reporting that "nearly a third of Syria's Christians, about 600,000, have found themselves with no choice but to flee the country, driven out by extremist groups like the Nusra Front and now ISIS."[3]*

*But many have stayed behind, like Mani and his wife. They chose to stay for one reason: there is an unbelievable and historic turn of Muslims to Jesus, and Mani's family—and those like them—believe they are called to be a part of it. Now they're seeing displaced Muslims, separated from the families who would normally pressure them to remain in Islam, showing interest in church and even making public conversions. Mani fishes in his pocket for a photo, beaming like a new father. It's a smiling family in traditional Islamic garb, the wife covered head to toe. "They came to Jesus and were baptized," he says. "She was baptized* in those clothes!"

*Mani has several invitations to immigrate to Europe. At home, he faces persecution, terrorism, deprivation, and constant threats. He stays on constant alert for danger. He's unhappy about the foreign aid provided to the militants that threaten him. But he readily accepts the humanitarian aid that helps his church care for hundreds of families in their area. He's one of the heroes who stays in harm's way with his entire young family because he sees the fields "white unto harvest." There are hundreds like him all across the Middle East.*

> A lot of pressure was on our family. Economic pressures. Security pressures. The main challenge was making the decision whether to stay in Syria or leave. Many people left our city, left the church, and went to other cities. Many

people traveled out of Syria. It would be easier to leave. People I know in Europe have called me, saying they have a place for me to stay.

Plus, the situation is very bad with the Jabhat al-Nusra circling the city. [Jabhat al-Nusra is an affiliate of al-Qaeda.] Once I was returning home, and on the way we came under fire. I didn't realize we were under fire, but when we came to a government checkpoint, they asked me about coming under fire on the road. I told them I never realized that. And they said, "You should have heard it! Go! Go fast!"

Jabhat al-Nusra knows my phone number too. They've sent me an SMS text that they are going to kill me. I asked the government to change my phone number, but they said no. But if someone sends me a new message, I can tell the government about this number texting me, and they said they will deal with the problem. So I've been praying.

But Jabhat al-Nusra knows a lot of information about me. They could capture me. For example, one time we baptized a Muslim man who received Jesus. Al-Nusra knows him. They know his name.

Another time, we were coming back home. On the road, there was a roadblock, so we chose to use another road through another village. On the way, we met a man and his family in their car as well. We joined together to travel because we knew Jabhat al-Nusra was in those villages on the road along the way.

We put the men in one car and the women and children in another car. We decided the car with the men would go ahead. That way if the car with the men were stopped, they would try to call the women and tell them to go back. When we started driving for only about one kilometer, a half-mile, I thought, *No, it's good to keep the families together in their own cars.*

So we changed again, and I said my car would go first. The checkpoint up ahead was antigovernment. A Jabhat al-Nusra man was wearing a mask. You could see just his eyes. They stopped me, and he put his weapon to my face. When he put the weapon to my face, my son started crying. When the man saw that my son kept crying and crying, he said, "This is a family, so it's okay if we don't check them." So we left.

Then the other car drove up. The same exact thing happened for them. If we had kept the men in the same car, we probably wouldn't have survived. Also, my ID card is southern territory, and that's a population who supports the government. This checkpoint was antigovernment. Because my ID card is from southern territory, it's very dangerous. And I am a Christian, and we are notorious for supporting the government. So I was a target for two reasons. This was a big, big problem, a double problem.

After that, I decided we needed to leave that area. My parents stayed behind. Soon after that Jabhat al-Nusra took over their area and started causing problems. Jabhat al-Nusra took my house key from my parents. They wanted to take the house to have for themselves. Nearby was a Christian village. They took all of the Christians' houses. Now there's mostly older people in there. Nearly no young people, because there is potential for the younger people to be captured and held as a ransom. Altogether they took around eighty homes.

Plus, the area near there had maybe ten more Christian villages. All of them are now under control of Jabhat al-Nusra. Some of the churches there were turned into mosques. Because I am a preacher, it is forbidden for me to return to my home village. I can't visit my parents. But I still go there once a month. I just cannot go direct, because if I go direct, I run into Jabhat al-Nusra.

In my village where we live now, we have three churches—evangelical, Catholic, and Orthodox. But we cannot open the churches. We cannot ring the bells. We cannot pray. Now I serve two churches in two different villages.

All of this was hard for us at the beginning. The security issue is very hard. The decision about if we should leave or not is very hard. My own parents and my wife struggled very hard. But finally, we felt God continuing to call us to stay. Now when we have problems, we feel that God is with us. It's not an easy choice though.

At the beginning of every month, we have a prayer meeting and then go and distribute aid. Around 100 to 150 people come to the meeting. A lot of people who come never knew we had a prayer meeting. They talk to us over Facebook, and some have even asked us to do it twice monthly! So now we are going to repair the church building that was damaged by the war.

Many people who come to us are displaced families, so we show them love, we listen to them, understand their problems, show our compassion for them. If they leave, we take their phone numbers and we still connect with them, talk to them. This is very important because they see that someone cares, someone is willing to hear about their problems.

Our church gives aid to the Christian families in our area—evangelical, Orthodox, and Catholic. If people didn't have this, many would starve. We provide medical aid as well. When someone is in the hospital, we help them and help provide money for it. Then they come back and stay connected with us and pray with us. All these ministries— people see them as very important. We've given people money to rent houses, money for transportation.

Now our church is full! We also have a small church in the other village where we minister, and about 100–125 people attend, so it is full too.

Many coming to Jesus are Muslims. In the past, it was very hard for Muslims to enter the church because they feared each other. Now there are so many displaced families that the Muslims who convert are not near their families. When they are separated, it is easier for them to come to faith because there is not as much pressure from family members. This makes it much easier for them to enter the church.

We have seen this in many cities in Syria. We see it happening outside of Syria. Many, many Muslims have come to Jesus. Many of them read the Bible, and they rejoice over it.

Yes, there is destruction and many problems. But on

the other side, you see many Muslims turning to God and coming to know Jesus.

It is much harder for Muslims than for Christians. Christians aren't being attacked as often. They are persecuted, but not as much as someone from a Muslim background. For a Muslim turning to Christianity, their own family attacks them and persecutes them.

In Syria there is a difference between being real Christians and being a Christian in name only. For those who come to real Christianity from Christianity in name only, they already understand things. They've read the Bible. They know the truth. For Muslims, it's much harder to turn to Jesus. I know a doctor. He traveled to Damascus to receive aid from a church. The church invited him to accept Jesus, and he believes now. He lost everything he had—his house, his clinic, everything.

Many Christians in Syria left. Most left for Europe. Most of the workers in our church and others—Sunday school teachers, youth workers—they left churches and traveled out of Syria. This was a challenge for us, for our ministries.

But many, many Muslims, Druze, or other Christians from other areas have come to our church. People from different sects are coming to Jesus. Because of our nation's problems, they try to find some comfort, so they start asking about Jesus as the one who can help them.

The displaced people who experience Jesus who are from Muslim backgrounds, when they return to their area, they need wisdom and grace so they can continue serving

Christ. We get their Facebook, WhatsApp, or other contact information. That way, if they come back to Syria, we can continue to serve them in church. If this war ends and they return to Syria, they can continue to be ministered to. We want to continue the ministry that they received wherever they went.

There is trouble, but God has disconnected many Muslim families so he can save the Muslims. Many Christians are fleeing, but we also know this is a great opportunity to turn people to Christ. **"**

## ALIYA  || *Kenya*

*Growing up as a Muslim in Kenya, Aliya repelled fifty—literally, fifty—marriage proposals in order to follow her own path. This angered her strict Muslim parents. But when they moved her and her siblings to America, Aliya knew she finally had an opportunity to pursue her own dreams. It was after she struck out on her own and moved to Texas that some neighbors came knocking on her door to invite her to a church home group. By this time, Aliya had married. Bowing to her parents' pressure, her husband had converted to Islam, and then to her horror, he became an extremist.*

*Regardless of the complexities of her situation, Aliya fell in love with Jesus because of neighbors who looked beyond her religion and ethnicity and saw her as someone in need of his love. Steadfast in their newfound faith, Aliya and her children are overcoming every challenge and following Jesus.*

"I was born in Kenya to Muslim parents. My mother is Pakistani/Afghani. My father is Indian/Iranian. In Africa, I had a very strict upbringing. I couldn't go out or wear makeup. I followed very strict rules of dress. They arranged a marriage for me when I was thirteen, but I refused to go through with it.

Every time we went to the mosque or any religious event, I didn't enjoy it. Muslims don't treat women well. Men are in the front, women in the back. My parents sent us as kids to the mosque to learn the Koran, but I grew up not understanding what I was reading. I felt lost and empty.

My parents were physically and emotionally abusive toward me. We moved to America when I was a teenager. After we moved, one day my sister who is eight years younger than me said, "I love you." I was seventeen years old, and it was the first time I had ever heard those words.

My parents kept trying to arrange a marriage for me in California with Pakistani men. I went through at least fifty marriage proposals, turning them all down. I just wanted to get an education and go to college, now that I had the opportunity in America.

My parents pressured me and said, "The only time you can leave is when you get married." But I insisted and got my MBA, then started a good career in California. Still, my parents kept pressuring me, and it always ended up in a fight. They were very narrow minded. Again and again they would tell me, "You need to get married!"

My brother ended up moving to Texas, so I followed

him. I met my husband there, but my family said he needed to be Muslim to marry me. So he agreed to convert to Islam. He did what they call taking the *shahadah*. That means he studied the Islamic Creed to convert to Islam.

This led to a whole new set of problems. We had lots of battles because of my husband converting. We were supposed to be Muslim but didn't have respect for Islam. And we didn't respect the Koran. It was very complicated. There were lots of battles.

We had our first son, then a second. After our second was born, every time we tried to pray the Islamic way, he would have a fit. He would scream and scream. But he would only do that if we were praying. It was the strangest thing.

Then my husband started talking about joining Al-Qaeda. He became an extremist. That's how he talks to this day.

One day, people across the street came over and invited us for dinner. My husband said, "We don't have to go." But I wanted to, so the kids and I went. When we got there, we found out it was a church gathering, a home group meeting. But we all got along right away. It was like love at first sight. I felt at home there.

I got close with a lady from that group, and she would invite me there every week. I would look forward to hearing them pray. I started seeing the prayers coming true. They would talk about what they learned at church that day. I would think about what they said all the time. It consumed me.

I started questioning my faith a lot and started doing research. *Why are these people so wonderful?* I would think. *What's their secret?* So I thought, *Maybe I should join a new mosque.* Maybe I just hadn't fit in at my parents' mosque.

But whatever I tried—learn Arabic, fit in—people pushed me away. Nobody made eye contact. It was suffocating me. Every time I went to the mosque, I would go back to my car and rip my scarf off. Every experience was bad.

Ten months into going to the new group, they talked about the light of Jesus. That's the difference. They had the light, and I didn't. So it clicked. That's the day I realized the truth. I couldn't sleep for two nights.

One night, something woke me up from my sleep. A force went through my soul. Almost right away it cleared up. I felt it was Jesus coming to save me. This made a big impact.

After learning about the love of Christ, I told my friend I needed a Bible. My friend said to start with Psalms. I started reading the Bible, and it grabbed ahold of my heart. I couldn't stop reading it. This is what I've been looking for all of my life! I knew this is the truth. This is God's Word! I read the Bible in a year. Then I took Bible classes. I find so much truth and depth in the Bible, so much unconditional love.

They had ladies' night at the church. I was scared to go. I knew I would like it too much, and then what might happen? There I heard Christian music for the first time.

The words were powerful. I started crying. I saw all the women worshiping. I never felt like that before. It was a very powerful night.

Another time at church, the sermon was about transformation. Soon after, I finally decided to receive Christ as my Savior. I became a Christian at my friend's house. I got baptized a few months later.

One year later, I felt a real tug to do mission work. I couldn't because I owned a bakery business. I couldn't take vacation. The next week, a lady walked into the bakery and said, "Sell me your bakery so you can follow your dreams!" That was so bizarre! I no longer had an excuse, so I was able to go on my first mission trip, to the Czech Republic.

My parents eventually found out that I became a Christian. Ironically, they were in the process of building a mosque. They disowned me. They said some very harsh things. They said, "You've made the worst decision. You're going to burn in hell for eternity. You can't come to our funerals, and we won't go to yours." The whole process was a hard choice, but now I was adamant that my kids grow up in Christianity.

It's been three years now, and I'm still trying to reconcile with my family. We started to make peace, but then all of a sudden they turned on me again and tried to convince me to come back to Islam. "You need to talk to a Muslim priest," they said.

There have been times that it hurts to go to church, knowing that it hurts my family. But my kids will say,

"Mom, please take us to church! We really want to go!" They give me the strength to keep going.

The pastor of my church suggested I get involved in an international student ministry. I lead a Bible study for them every Friday. It's very encouraging to see new students' faces light up. Just like mine did. 🙶

Mani's and Aliya's stories illustrate just how ripe the fields are for harvest, particularly in the Muslim world. But participating in the harvest will require risk and sacrifice on our part—which explains why Jesus says, "The harvest is great, but the workers are few." So we must "pray to the Lord who is in charge of the harvest; ask him to send more workers into his fields" (Matthew 9:37-38, NLT).

The Martyr's Oath statement that frames this chapter is "May those around me see the face of Jesus reflected in me," but too often our version is something like "May those around me see the face of Jesus reflected in me as long as it doesn't make me uncomfortable or unpopular or unsafe or poor or less powerful or less important." We add so many caveats that we can miss our opportunity to hear the call of Jesus sending *us* to be part of the harvest. I understand that each of us has different gifts, opportunities, responsibilities, life stages, and on and on. It might not be possible for you to travel overseas to work with Muslim refugees or to put yourself in danger in the world's riskiest places for Christ. And that's okay. But regardless of where you are, you *can* be part of this worldwide movement to introduce those seeking God to Jesus.

Because we're so terrified of the violence of extremists, we can be uneasy or even *hostile* when we see people wearing traditional Islamic clothing shopping in the grocery store or sitting next to us on the plane. But as David Garrison so powerfully observes, "This is not the day to fear, fight, hate or kill Muslims. . . . This is their day of salvation. God loves them—if you want to be on God's side in this day, be a part of what God's doing."[4]

The admonition to treat "strangers" with love and dignity is as old as the Torah. God declares, "The alien who resides with you shall be to you as the citizen among you; you shall love the alien as yourself, for you were aliens in the land of Egypt: I am the LORD your God" (Leviticus 19:34, NRSV).

In the United States, one of the blackest moments in our history occurred in 1939, when the *St. Louis*, a cruise ship full of more than nine hundred German Jewish refugees fleeing Nazi persecution, was denied permission to dock in the United States.[5] Forced to return to Europe, "254 of them were eventually killed in the Holocaust."[6]

If you're a Christian who takes the Bible seriously, then you cannot do anything but welcome and show kindness to refugees.

Period.

Full stop.

Any other attitude or response is entirely unbiblical, and it grieves God himself.

In our times of fear and global unrest, one of the key indicators of the seriousness with which we follow Jesus is how we treat those different from us.

The flow of refugees into this country offers an *unprecedented* opportunity for witness:

- It is difficult to witness to Muslims overseas, but *easy* to do here. In parts of the Middle East and North Africa, it is usually illegal to witness and illegal for Muslims to convert, and as we've seen, these offenses can be punishable by death. By contrast, here we are free in this country to love and to preach, and those of other faiths are free to receive love and trust Christ.
- Some Muslims in the Middle East are trapped. As much as they may be drawn to Jesus, their family members and friends will turn violently against them without fear of repercussions. By contrast, here they are free to follow Jesus, and while their families may vehemently disagree with their decision, they may not use violence to intimidate them.
- When you witness to others, it's easier for them to witness to their families and friends—both here and there.

But I have to tell you, your testimony of Jesus will be effective and authentic only when it comes from your heart. You mustn't simply make a decision to share your faith to the Islamic world. It must begin with loving Muslims—*legitimately* loving them.

In my trips to Muslim countries all around our world, I've always found the most hospitable and kind people. I've found friends who disagree with me, and I disagree with them, but we love one another with a genuine friendship. I recognize that terrorism and extremism has killed more Muslims than anyone else, and I feel sorry for them. I'm heartbroken for them, and I want so badly for them to know peace and security. Sometimes I'd rather spend time with Muslims than with Christians. I even know many Muslims who love Jesus, and I love many Muslims!

It goes further. All the work I've done to help Christians in the Middle East began with the Islamic community, not the Christian community. The king of Jordan—a Muslim and a direct descendant of Muhammad—convened a small meeting of global Christian leaders out of his concern for persecuted Christians. He asked us to help, and I have. I've helped raise more than $25 million to help Christians stay in the Middle East or to rebuild their lives when they've chosen to leave.[7]

It all began with a Muslim man who loved his Christian neighbors. Their witness of Jesus in the Middle East made them attractive to him, and he wanted to help them. He couldn't imagine a Middle East without them.

Here's the news flash: Jesus loves that Muslim king every bit as much as he loves those Christians who face persecution.

Jesus loves Muslims as much as he loves you.

Teach that to your children and to your church, but first, believe it in your heart. We must be prepared to share Jesus with others— regardless of the cost—whether around the world or in our own backyards.

# CHAPTER 13

# I HAVE TAKEN UP MY CROSS

*The message of the cross is foolishness to those who are perishing,*
*but to us who are being saved it is the power of God.*

1 CORINTHIANS 1:18

**FOLLOWERS OF JESUS** are not at war with any system, and the Bible teaches us to be good citizens and to submit to our governments. The apostle Paul issued this command to the church in Rome: "Everyone must submit to governing authorities. For all authority comes from God, and those in positions of authority have been placed there by God" (Romans 13:1, NLT). In addition, we are specifically taught to "make it your goal to live a quiet life, minding your own business and working with your hands, just as we instructed you before. Then people who are not believers will respect the way you live, and you will not need to depend on others" (1 Thessalonians 4:11-12, NLT).

Yet Communist regimes have singled Christians out for persecution, imprisonment, deportation, and execution for over a hundred years. A key tool of their repression is confiscation of anything valuable, in addition to imprisonment, extortion, shaming, and various forms of abuse and marginalization.

From the beginning, Communism has set its sights on the extermination of Christianity. Vladimir Lenin, one of the architects of Communism in Russia, wrote:

> Religion is the opium of the people—this dictum by Marx is the corner-stone of the whole Marxist outlook on religion. Marxism has always regarded all modern religions and churches, and each and every religious organisation, as instruments of bourgeois reaction that serve to defend exploitation and to befuddle the working class.[1]

Yet the atheism that was supposed to allow people to break their shackles has instead led them straight to the gallows. As Joseph Stalin is reported to have said, "The death of one man is a tragedy. The death of millions is a statistic." This is the legacy of Communism—multiplied millions murdered,[2] more than any other ideology at any other time by far. Communism has killed far more people than Islamic jihadism. Yet at its heart is the same persecution of those who follow Jesus.

When it comes to power, the Chinese Communist Party sees Christianity as a risk—any organization that claims ultimate allegiance, is international, and is growing quickly is perceived as a threat. This is especially true when that organization is religious. Chinese Communism has not let go of its allegiance to atheism: "In 1955, Chinese Communist leader Zhou Enlai declared, 'We Communists are atheists.' In 2014, the Communist Party of China reaffirmed that members of their party must be atheists."[3] The freedom of religion remains viciously restricted in China.

In April 2016, President Xi Jinping "urged the ruling Communist Party to 'resolutely guard against overseas infiltrations via religious means.'"[4] As Christianity is on track to become the majority faith in China by the end of the twenty-first century, the number of Christians already exceeds the number of Communist Party members. As the number of Communist Party members becoming Christians grows, the anxiety of the Communist government grows.

The government's response has been to remove crosses from church buildings and in some cases to destroy the church buildings too.

This isn't happening only in China. I recently received a video from my good friend Yvette Isaac, an Egyptian television personality, containing the testimonies of Christians in Syria. The video is heartbreaking. Yvette interviewed priests who told of how one of the very first things that ISIS did was to destroy the crosses on tops of churches.

There's something about the cross. The enemy hates that cross. It's personal. It's a reminder that he has been defeated and he will be ultimately defeated.

## JOE || *China*

*Joe has been protesting the destruction of crosses in China for a couple of years now, but Christians differ on how to handle the situation. Joe is calm and pensive, mild mannered, educated, articulate. His own church's cross was destroyed. But in a neighboring town, he watched how Christians withstood the government's advances. In a miraculous turn of events, they repelled the government and saved their cross. Later, the church leaders were arrested. Undeterred, the Christians appealed to Beijing and won the leaders' freedom. Along with their release, local officials begged them not to sue. The Christians turned right around and offered to pay the officials' legal fees. They took seriously the words "bless those who persecute you" (Romans 12:14, NLT), and their display of Christian grace and forgiveness glorified the Lord in the eyes of their persecutors.*

" In the past month, the government has torn down the rest of the crosses in our province. It's been their goal for a while. Last year, government representatives and "security guards" were contracted to take down the symbol of Christianity all across the province. If it's a big cross, they'll bring in large equipment to tear it down. My church's cross was taken down in 2015. Many more were taken down this year in a cluster of local congregations. Regardless, we rely on our God.

I started getting involved in protesting this issue in 2014 when it began to arise. We have two lines of thought about how the destruction started. For one, perhaps the party secretary in our province is coordinating these efforts to please the prime minister and solidify his political position. The other is that there has been direct permission from the prime minister to do this. However, a friend has assured me that the central bureau of the party has no interest in tearing down crosses.

The government has encountered pushback. They have

had international pressure from Britain, France, Germany, and the US. Among Chinese Christians, there have been two responses to this government overreach. One line of thinking is, "We don't have the power to fight the Communist Party." The second line is to say, "We don't fear the Communist Party. We depend on God." In this view, folks tell their local government they will protest these actions in Beijing.

For example, in the town of Tiashun, the government bragged that they were going to tear down a church cross. But the brothers and sisters of that congregation stood together around their church building. When one thousand people from the government came and confronted them, it felt like an army. Nevertheless, they were strong in their faith, and they blocked the government from coming in.

The government wanted to make an example of them. The next time government officials came, they brought officials from other towns, up to ten thousand people to watch what was about to unfold. But once again, the church members stood there singing hymns, singing Scripture. After a whole day, the government gave up trying to take down the cross. Late that night, they tried again. The day was completely clear, but when they came again at night, a thunderstorm disrupted their plans.

Later on, arrest notices were sent for twenty leaders of that church. When they would use their ID cards, stores would report them to the local government, and many of them were detained. Some of them were bailed out, but others refused to be bailed out. It was unlawful detainment, so their fellow church members appealed to Beijing and tried to negotiate the situation with the government. Then the local government finally said they would release them but asked, "Just please don't sue us." The church told them, "We will not."

God's name was greatly glorified through all of this. The government thought taking down the cross would destroy the church, but the opposite has happened. Many have been willing to give their life for their faith. Many journalists have interviewed us, from all over the world. This has been a wake-up call for the church. Faith has been revived. 〞

## HAN AND ZHANG || China

*"We are not afraid to die," Han states. "We don't care. We just continue serving the Lord." With a big grin, Zhang adds, "I'm prepared to die!" Through years of harassment and false imprisonment of their pastor, their church continued to meet. "We grew bolder in our faith," they both agree. When their pastor came home from prison, they said, "Before, we were meeting in the basement, but now we started meeting in the sun."*

*It is impossible to find even the "smell of smoke" on the two people sipping tea, even though they continue to go through incredible fire. They just have unrelenting, persevering joy. Han and Zhang are from a rural area in northwest China. They are relatives, bonded by blood as well as by common experience. Dark-skinned with a huge white smile, Han sets his jaw when he talks. He is resolute, unable to be shaken from his faith. Zhang is much shorter but carries a family resemblance. She never stops smiling. Even when speaking about their difficulties, she speaks with surprising cheerfulness.*

*They hold their aromatic tea and speak softly of one of their family members who was imprisoned and beaten. He became unrecognizable, deformed, and pale. They continually face harassment from the government. They have been detained, had their church materials confiscated, and have been falsely accused. Yet they represent the best of Christianity, believers whose faith grows ever deeper, even in the times of severe testing.*

## HAN

" My father-in-law is my pastor. Over fifteen years ago, the local government disturbed our gathering in a basement and told us we couldn't sing out loud. Our pastor was detained for fifteen days, then later detained again—three times in one month. He was brought to "drinking teas," which means interrogation by the government.

They banned the pastor from traveling outside the country, and then even from parts of China. They confiscated our church materials—Bibles, hymnal, musical instruments—even without a proper search warrant. He had an outside business, but he had to shut it down. Finally, they charged him with "espionage," "overthrow of the government," and said he had "ties with anti-government factions."

Schoolteachers were instructed to watch the students

whose parents attended our church. Two of the children were forced to drop out of school, a problem that has lingered because later in life, they have not been able to find jobs.

About ten years ago, our pastor was arrested again and imprisoned for a year. There was no reason, no sentence, no trial. He was put in a "black prison," which means it's an illegal prison and doesn't have a fair legal process. He couldn't be seen by anyone. He was severely beaten by the prison warden. He became a ghostly image of his former self because he never saw light. His hands became deformed. He looked terrible.

Yet when he returned, he had a new zeal. He had even more courage than before. The church continued gathering, and we grew bolder in our faith. Before, we were meeting in the basement, but now we started meeting in the sun. With confidence and boldness, we would praise and worship outside.

In the past two years, many police officials came to take pictures of our church. A year ago, my wife and I were teaching Sunday school and were illegally arrested. This happened once before, eight years ago. Someone reported me to the police, so they interrogated me overnight, then detained me. On this second arrest, all the children in the Sunday school were brought into the police station with us—children as young as three years old. Their parents had to come to claim them. The only way the parents could get their children released was by signing a statement that they would never send their children to our Sunday school again.

My wife and I were kept for eleven days. A coworker

tried to reason with the police. But we were charged with "falsely using religion to threaten the security of the society." The officials forced us to sign a statement saying we would "not commit the same crime again."

We worked with a lawyer from Beijing to sue the police chief for unlawful practices, but the suit was rejected. But we don't care. We are not afraid to die. We just continue serving the Lord. We are still being watched closely to this day, but this is a typical situation of many house churches. Maybe I could be killed—who knows? I've told my family to prepare for me to be in prison for two years. We have things in order, just in case something were to happen.

The biggest blessing is how we've grown stronger in our faith. We're not afraid of the government. What we've gone through binds us together. Before, we used to hide, but after suffering, now we have a church building. The church body is getting bigger. We are on a major traffic route, so we receive missionaries from many places.

We are very active in our community. We are a beacon to our neighbors. For example, we offer funeral services to the community. Before all of these events, we didn't do these things. 99

## ZHANG

66 We invited a missionary from Singapore to visit our congregation. One morning, we gathered together early to

pray. It was raining and we thought we saw lightning outside, but it was the police taking pictures. They crashed
the meeting. "Stop singing!" they said.

The officials surrounded us and crammed us into a
van—almost fifty people. It was a long walk in the rain
to the police van, but the church members were laughing
and smiling the whole time. Through all of this, our spirits
were not crushed.

The ironic part is that our guest speaker was speaking
about enduring persecution that day. We got a real-life
example far sooner than we could have imagined. Forty-
four people were detained for only one day. The other four
were detained for a whole month. The missionary from
Singapore was sent home.

One elder was abused tremendously in prison. He was
raped. He was often sleep deprived. They would pull his
hair and his genitals. He was on the verge of committing
suicide, but the next day, they set him free. He passed away
last year. He was a very active evangelist for the faith.

I have told my husband what to do if I am detained. I
said, "If the police give you any trouble, just say you will
divorce me. And if you are able to visit me, bring me warm
clothes."

He knows I am prepared to die. ''

The cross has been a powerful symbol of Christianity from the very
beginning. An instrument of torture and execution, it has become

a symbol of our salvation. Because of Jesus Christ's death on the cross for us, our sin debt is paid. The cross is a reminder that, in Jesus, God the Father no longer holds our sins against us.

But the cross is also a reminder to us that we must "offer [our] bodies as a living sacrifice, holy and pleasing to God" (Romans 12:1). Jesus told his disciples, "Whoever wants to be my disciple must deny themselves and take up their cross daily and follow me" (Luke 9:23). In order to follow Jesus, we must deny ourselves. We must put our sinful nature—with all its ambitions and desires and fears—to death. "For whoever wants to save their life will lose it, but whoever loses their life for me will save it" (Luke 9:24).

It is no accident that those who persecute Christians want to destroy the cross. Beyond its symbolism of Christ's eventual triumph—when "all his enemies" will be "put . . . under his feet" (1 Corinthians 15:25)—the cross lets earthly rulers know that Christians answer to a higher authority than them. Especially in totalitarian regimes, which demand unwavering allegiance, the cross is a threat. While Christians must submit to the governing authorities, our submission can go only so far.

And because of its precious symbolism, Christians around the world would rather die than give up the cross. This idea can seem foreign to us in the United States. Yet the symbol of the cross has so saturated our culture—it adorns necklaces and social-media profiles and car bumpers—that many of us no longer *see* it. It's just part of the backdrop. But for many of our persecuted brothers and sisters, the cross is their salvation, it is their life, and they love the cross. Wearing the cross will cost them something. Having the cross tattooed on their hands or arms will cost them something. Having the cross on their churches will cost them something. The cross is a public statement of where their true allegiance lies, and it is a public statement that no matter the cost, they will follow Jesus.

The cross should be a reminder to all of us that following Jesus will cost us something—our very lives. "Taking up our cross" means conditioning ourselves to understand that sacrifice is a regular experience. Sacrifice is the front line of a war we have with ourselves and our sinful nature. Sacrifice is the beginning of service and the cost of becoming a witness to the world!

Nobody wins this war in the blink of an eye or in a single circumstance. It's something we'll be engaged in constantly, for the rest of our lives. We're going to have to die daily—every single day. We need to die daily because we're not *recovered* addicts. We're *recovering* addicts, and what we're addicted to is ourselves—our selfishness, our desires, our safety.

Zhang's final words in her story are an expression of what all of us who claim Jesus as our Lord should believe: "I am prepared to die." We should be prepared to die because the central symbol of our faith reminds us of Jesus' death and of his call to "follow me."

# CHAPTER 14

# I HAVE LAID EVERYTHING ELSE DOWN

*[Moses chose] rather to be mistreated with the people of God than*
*to enjoy the fleeting pleasures of sin. He considered the reproach*
*of Christ greater wealth than the treasures of Egypt, for he was*
*looking to the reward. By faith he left Egypt, not being afraid of the*
*anger of the king, for he endured as seeing him who is invisible.*

HEBREWS 11:25-27, ESV

**THE DESCRIPTION OF MOSES** given above is an illustration of what it means to "lay everything else down." Laying everything else down implies a trade-off: you lose one thing and gain another.

For unbelievers, sacrificing anything for Christianity seems incomprehensible. Even for some Christians, when they see the price believers around the world are paying to follow Jesus, they balk at the cost. "Was sacrifice really necessary? Isn't there a win-win compromise to be found?"

But while compromise on some issues may be possible and even necessary, the Bible speaks in black-and-white terms when it comes to following Jesus—and it does so often. Jesus says, "No one can serve two masters. . . . You cannot serve both God and money" (Matthew 6:24). And the apostle Paul writes, "You cannot drink the cup of the Lord and the cup of demons too; you cannot have a part in both the Lord's table and the table of demons" (1 Corinthians 10:21). There are some cases where it is simply not possible to compromise.

Throughout this book we've seen examples of believers paying huge costs for their faith in Christ, yet each one of them has counted the price paid worth it. In this chapter, I want to share two more stories—those of Ahmed and Rayna—two believers who have paid a huge price to follow Jesus but who consider that price a bargain.

 **AHMED** || *Iran*

*Ahmed grew up in a strict Muslim family. When he had no hope for the guilt he felt about his sin, he attempted to take his own life. After he survived the suicide attempt, his brother suggested he attend church. He investigated, and he liked it, but he couldn't grasp what it meant to follow Jesus.*

*Ahmed reached the point that turns many Muslims into followers of Jesus. He had a revelation: "The mullah had no answer for my guilt, but Jesus did: he had shed his blood."*

*The decision to follow Jesus rocked Ahmed. He could not stop telling people about him, even though he lived under a strict extremist government. He was a part of creating a house church, which spawned more churches.*

*Ahmed married a beautiful woman who also loved Jesus, and*

*the adventure began. He and his new wife landed in prison. Twice.*
*And they never stopped ministering.*

"I was born into a fanatical Muslim family in Tehran. When
I was a child, my parents would wake me up every day at
5:00 a.m. and say, "Come on, get up and say your prayers.
If you don't, God will punish you." If I didn't keep the
annual fast, they would say the same thing: "God will
punish you." At home, my mother and sister wore the veil.
That's the sort of devout Islamic family I grew up in.

When I became a young man, I committed a sin and
felt very guilty. The guilt would not go. I thought the
best thing to do was to go and see a mullah to get help.
I talked with him for hours, asking him to tell me how to
find peace. At the end, all he could say was, "Go away
and don't sin again."

"Look," I said, "I committed that sin a month ago. I
haven't committed that sin again. But I still feel terrible."
The mullah had nothing to say to me. I went home full of
despair.

Then one day I found an answer. When there was
nobody in our house, I went around the house collecting
every pill I could find. I swallowed them all in one go. I
wanted to die. I became unconscious. But it wasn't the end.
I opened my eyes in a hospital bed, and a doctor was looking
down at me. He said, "You're a miracle. You should be dead."

I thought, *I wish I was dead.* I went back home still carrying my despair.

One day, my brother called me. He had become a Christian. He said, "Go to church." I managed to find a church in Tehran. I went, unsure what to expect. The worship moved me. The preaching spoke to me. So I kept on going, but I did not understand the gospel.

Then one evening it all opened up for me. God in Christ had given his life for my sins. The mullah had no answer for my guilt, but Jesus did. He had shed his blood. I knelt in God's presence, and tears of joy poured down my face. I had never had a moment like that in my life. I was so happy that when the meeting was over, I ran down the street.

I knew there were millions of others like me who were depressed. I knew they had no answer to their sin in their religion. So I had to share Jesus with them. I talked about his forgiveness wherever I went.

Once I was the only passenger in a taxi, and I started telling the driver, Ali, about my life. I told him about my past, how tired I was, and how much I was in sin. And I told him how Jesus had saved me from suicide. When I finished, Ali looked at me and asked me to open the dashboard. I did. It was full of pills.

"This morning," Ali said, "I vowed to kill myself. I was like you, without hope. You were going to be my last passenger."

I said, "Wait, I need to tell you more." After I had shared, I prayed for Ali, as I have since prayed for hundreds and hundreds of Iranians who are depressed. I then gave him a New Testament.

Ali looked at me with eyes full of hope: "It is no accident that you are my passenger today."

Now I saw myself as a soldier, and I knew that soldiers needed to be trained. I understood that an organization was training people in a country neighboring Iran to share the gospel and plant churches. So I went. After three months I returned to Iran better equipped to share the gospel.

I would go to the street and talk with people about Jesus. People were so ready. They would believe right there in the street! I would make appointments to speak with them in a public park. As I grew to know them, I would invite them to my house. And so a house church was born.

As more people came to Christ, they would share with others. Soon there was no place in the home. So more house churches were born.

We knew this was illegal to share Jesus and start house churches, but Jesus said, "Go," so we did. We went to other cities and planted churches there. And so we continued.

I married a beautiful woman. She was very faithful and full of love. Four months after we were married, on Christmas Day, there was a knock on our door. It was the security police. They came into our home. They took our computers, our passports, our papers. They took me away. Four policemen escorted me in a car to prison. They told my wife she needed to come to an office later to answer questions. There, she was arrested.

For forty-five days I was in solitary confinement. It was

the worst place. There was no one to talk to and no one to witness to. It was a small room with just one window. Once a week, I was allowed to shower. And once a week for fifteen minutes, I was allowed outside to look at the sky.

But after forty-five days, they moved me to a larger cell. There were fifteen other people. That was a very good place. They were all tired of life and open to the gospel. I told them all about Jesus. After seventy-eight days, she and I were both set free. They said, "We are only releasing you temporarily. You must stay in the city and come back when we call you."

A year later, they called us. They asked me if I was a Muslim or a Christian. I said, "I'm a Christian." They asked my wife, and she also said she's a Christian. I was sentenced to six years in prison. My wife was sentenced to five years. Again they sent us home and said they would soon be calling us.

When we arrived home, we decided we should leave Iran. We had no passports, so we had to leave over the mountains. We arrived in a town where there was no Persian-speaking church. We continued to evangelize, and soon a church was planted there.

My mother, who was still a very devout Muslim, came to visit me. She stayed in our home, and because our home was also the house church, she heard much about Jesus and the gospel. And there, in this city where I was a refugee, my mother gave her life to Jesus. Other members of my family also believed. I was overjoyed.

In time, we traveled to another city. We started a

church there with forty Iranians from a Muslim background. We met in a home. But after a few weeks of witnessing, we no longer fit in the home. So we went to two services. We kept evangelizing. Soon we no longer fit in the house, even with two services.

We decided to rent a bigger space. We found one that would fit two hundred people. I thought surely this would be more space than we would need. But in a few months' time, we were overcrowded again. Again we went to two services.

In just under a year in that one city, we went from forty to over four hundred members. And the church continues to grow.

It was during my time as a refugee that God gave me the verse Romans 8:28: "And we know that for those who love God all things work together for good." My story includes much suffering, persecution, and trials. Much of it has been painful. But God remains faithful. And he is working for good. 〟

## RAYNA || *Algeria*

*Rayna's sister said, "If you were back in Algeria, you know that your head would be cut off. You have lost your soul."*

*The sadness is unmistakable in Rayna's voice. She wants desperately to be reconciled to her family. But coming from a strict culture of Islam in Algeria, her family considers her love of Jesus unacceptable. It doesn't surprise her, because she sees her former religion as shame based and knows her family cares a lot about what others think.*

*And she really didn't mean to become a follower of Jesus. She was trying to convert her coworkers to Islam when she found herself wrestling with the religion she was raised in. She read God's Word and experienced the power of the Holy Spirit, and she was changed. She is devoted to following Jesus now, even though it has meant persecution by her own family.*

" I was a devout Muslim. As a teenager, I started to be really, really conservative. Then I lost my dad. This was the first time I felt real fear. I feared death, so I wanted to get closer to God. I started wearing the cover, the hijab, and started staying away from friends that were not covering. I started reading more of the Koran.

My mom was my world. She said we would go to the United States, and that changed my life plans. What Algerians see on TV is what we perceive Christians are like in the West. So when I came to America as a teenager, I was afraid of meeting people. I was dedicated to my religion, and my perception of Western culture was that it was "Christianity," where people didn't care and did whatever they wanted. I tried not to have close friends in school. I would be kind and say, "Hi," but I would think, *May God protect me from the infidels in the US.*

I moved away from home and studied finance and economics in college. In college, I got a job in a chemistry lab and started getting to know people. They happened to be a good Christian group. They would talk about God. One guy would bring his Bible every single day. These people would talk about Jesus and about the *love* of God. This started to make me rethink what Christianity is.

As I started to get close to them, I thought, *I need to do a better job to get them to become Muslim.* I would go to Muslim workshops. An Imam there used to be a Christian worship pastor, but he became a Muslim. At that mosque, I would talk with females who also were Christian but became Muslims. We were *talking* about Islam, but these women were Americans who had never been in a Muslim country. We'd talk about women's rights and that a Muslim woman would have to accept that her husband would marry four women. This was my first time realizing that if I were a Muslim, I couldn't pick and choose. I had to believe *everything* the Koran said. It was the first time I had to deal with reality and the fact that Islam gives no rights to females.

I began studying the Koran more in depth from that point on to do some critical thinking. Inside, I knew God existed. I never gave up on that. But I questioned if the man I would marry could really have the ability to take me to hell or not. I had a huge problem with that line of thinking. So I said, "God, show me who you are."

At a friend's house, one of the roommates had his Bible on the table all the time. I would debate with them. Finally, I started taking the Bible without letting them know and bringing it back. I wanted to know about Jesus and what he said. I noticed the words of Jesus were written in red. *Oh, that must be important*, I thought. His words were very inspiring and comforting, particularly about for-giveness. Just from reading the Word, I got understanding from the Holy Spirit that Jesus was God.

A month or so after I became a Christian, I decided to call my mother and tell her. At first, she thought I was just joking. "So you are telling me God has a son?" she said. She just laughed. It was a shock to her, so I had to call her back. It was just very dramatic and shocking for her. But she seemed to be okay with it for about the first year.

Then I told my sister by e-mail. My sister said, "If you were back in Algeria, you know that your head would be cut off. You have lost your soul." Later my mom got worse about my conversion. I'm her daughter, and it's important for her not to have shame in her community. She said to my sister one time, "At least she isn't using drugs." That meant I didn't go totally off the deep end.

Now my sister hasn't spoken to me for seven years. When I had a baby, I sent an e-mail saying she was an aunt. She responded and said, "May Allah bless him." My niece saw on Facebook that I was wearing a cross. She wrote me, "You need to take this cross off." I said, "This is what I believe." My family cannot accept my faith, but I never have a single doubt that God can reach them, too. 99

Prison. Family strife. Having to leave home. These seem like a high price, and indeed they are. But both Ahmed and Rayna paid them happily for the joy of knowing Jesus.

When counting the cost of following Jesus, it is easy for us to forget that paying a high price for something is foolishness only if what you get isn't worth it. If you paid several thousand dollars for a piece of costume jewelry, people might legitimately judge that you overpaid. If you paid the same several thousand dollars for a piece of beachfront property in Southern California, those same people might congratulate you on the bargain. Costs are relative.

I wonder if we've lost sight of the value of our salvation and of knowing Jesus. The apostle Paul—who had much to lose by following Jesus—put it this way: "Whatever were gains to me I now consider loss for the sake of Christ. What is more, I consider everything a loss because of the surpassing worth of knowing Christ Jesus my Lord, for whose sake I have lost all things. I consider them garbage, that I may gain Christ and be found in him" (Philippians 3:7-9). For Paul, being found in Christ was worth the price of losing his former accomplishments.

So I wonder again: Have we lost sight of the value of knowing Jesus?

Before we can even consider taking the Martyr's Oath, it's important that we know the value and the cost of our faith. Our lives can be so full of distractions and entertainment that it's difficult to know what we've paid and whether it's worth it. And this is where I think some other Christian traditions can help us gain perspective. For American Christians, where our default trajectory is comfort and safety, sometimes it is necessary for us to *choose* discomfort and sacrifice and even suffering in order to identify with Christ and with our brothers and sisters who are suffering in the world. Shortly after the passage quoted above, Paul explains, "I want to know Christ—yes, to know the power of his resurrection and participation in his sufferings" (Philippians 3:10). Part of knowing Jesus is participating in his sufferings, "becoming like him in his death, and so, somehow, attaining to the resurrection from the dead" (verses 10-11). To know the Resurrection, we have to know his death. And that involves sacrifice.

But where do we begin? One thing my family does that has helped us recalibrate to a mind-set of sacrifice is to try and practice the Sabbath. In most normal times, from sundown on Friday to sundown on Saturday, we separate ourselves from the world and from work. There's a reason. The Sabbath was instituted at Creation. It wasn't introduced in the law. In the Exodus story, God says that the Sabbath is a *gift* to humanity (see Exodus 16:29), and part of this gift is reconnecting with the Creator. So in my family, we turn our phones off, we unplug, and we do what we can to remain present where we are.

We weren't designed to always be distracted, to have our whims satisfied instantly, to live at such a fast pace. It's no wonder we're not understanding the deep things of God or taking martyr's oaths or making sacrifices for the Kingdom. For many of us, we worship our cell phones—our connection to the world. The way we live seamlessly in the digital world is the way we ought to live seamlessly in the Kingdom. Paul tells us to "pray without ceasing" (1 Thessalonians 5:17, ESV)—we should always be "connected" to God the way many of us are constantly connected to the Internet. The Internet is always there, and we can always get what we need, and our lives are integrated into it. And that's the way we're supposed to be plugged into the Kingdom; it ought to be that seamless. We *ought* to be that connected, and yet we aren't.

So when we consider whether we've already laid everything

down or are ready to, let me suggest to you that a good first step might be to unplug from everything else.

Turn off your cell phone. It seems like a simple thing, an infantile suggestion. Yet it is not. It is killing your soul.

As much as you're able, go somewhere you can be by yourself and talk to God. The spiritual disciplines—prayer, Bible reading, fasting, and so on—can be helpful here, as they teach us to intentionally sacrifice something for the sake of Christ. They are baby steps on the road to sacrificing greater things.

And, in sacrificing, I truly believe that we will find he is worth whatever price he has called us to pay.

# CHAPTER 15

# I WILL FOLLOW AND LOVE JESUS UNTIL THE END

*I have fought the good fight, I have finished the race, and I have remained faithful. And now the prize awaits me—the crown of righteousness, which the Lord, the righteous Judge, will give me on the day of his return.*

2 TIMOTHY 4:7-8, NLT

**THE NUNS DRAPE THEMSELVES** in the familiar white habit with blue trim, the same worn by their famous predecessor, Mother Teresa. The young women come from all over the world. When they first come together, their robes might be the only thing they have in common. But in the mission where they are assigned, they soon also share a love of the people they serve.

On the morning of March 4, 2016, five young women went to mass as usual. Afterward they had breakfast together where they worked—at the Missionaries of Charity home for the elderly in Aden, Yemen. Then they began their work. The elderly and sick in wheelchairs and beds dotted the sparse interior of the home. The young nuns knew each person and knew just how to help them.

But this was no ordinary morning. What happened after breakfast was written by one nun, Sister Rio, and her words were e-mailed to me by a Catholic friend. Except it wasn't typed as I've given it to you below. It was written by hand and in English—her account of her sisters' martyrdom, which she witnessed while hiding in the refrigerator room.[1]

## THE MARTYRED NUNS OF 2016 || *Yemen*

" The sisters had mass and breakfast as usual. At 8:00 a.m. they all prayed once again and all 5 went to the Home. At 8:30 a.m. ISIS came dressed in blue and killed the guard and the driver.

Five young Ethiopian men (Christians) began running to tell the sisters ISIS was here to kill them. The men were killed one by one. They tied them to trees, shot them in the head and then smashed their heads.

The sisters ran two by two in different directions. "Don't kill the sisters! Don't kill the sisters!" yelled some of the staff including the cook of fifteen years. So, ISIS killed them too.

They caught Sr. Judit and Sr. Reginette first, tied them, shot them in the head, and smashed their heads. When the sisters ran in different directions Sr. Sally ran to the convent to try and warn Father Tom. They caught Sr. Anselm and Sr. Marguerite, tied them, shot them in the head and smashed their heads in the sand. Meanwhile Sr. Sally could not get to the convent. It is not clear how many ISIS men were there. She saw all the sisters and helpers killed. The ISIS men were already getting to the convent so she went in the Refrigerator Room since the door was open. These ISIS men were everywhere searching for her, as they knew there were five of them. At least three times they came into the Refrigerator Room. She did not hide but remained standing behind the door—they never saw her. This is miraculous.

A neighbor saw them put Fr. Tom in their car. They did not find any trace of Father anywhere. All the religious articles were smashed and destroyed—Our Lady, Crucifix, altar, Tabernacle, lectionary stand—even their prayer books and Bibles.

At around 10:00 a.m. the ISIS men finished and left. Sr. Sally came to get the bodies of the sisters. She got them all. She also went to the medical patients in the facility to see if they were OK. All were OK. Not one was hurt. [ISIS came to kill the nuns, not the residents of the facility they cared for.]

The son of the woman who was the cook ([whom] ISIS killed) was calling her on her cell phone. Since she was not answering, he called the police and he went with the police there and found this great massacre. The police and son arrived at 10:30 a.m.

The police tried to take Sr. Sally out of there—she refused to leave because the patients were crying, "Don't leave us, stay with us!" But the police forced her to go with them because ISIS knew there were five sisters, and they were convinced that they would not stop until they killed her too. There was not enough room in the mortuary for the sisters' bodies.

Sr. Sally told Sr. Rio that she is so sad because she is alone and did not die with her sisters. Sr. Rio told her God wanted a witness and told her, "Who would have found the sisters bodies and who would ever tell us what happened? God wants us to know."

Sr. Sally told Sr. Rio that every day Fr. Tom told them, "Let us be ready for martyrdom."

ISIS wants to take over and exterminate any Christian presence. They were the only Christian presence and ISIS wants to get rid of all Christianity. So they are real martyrs—dead because they are Christians. They could have died so many times in the war but God wanted it to be clear they are martyrs for their faith.

The police are trying to get Sr. Sally out because ISIS will just keep after her until they kill her. She is fully surrendered and told Sr. Rio—whatever God wants. She said the other Muslims are so respectful of her. She said to pray that the blood of the sisters will be the seed for peace in the Middle East and to stop ISIS.

They were so faithful. They were in the right place at the right time and were ready when the Bridegroom came. 🙲

The killing of Christians only amplifies the gospel. And it inspires other Christians to greater service. When missionaries Jim Elliot, Ed McCully, Roger Youderian, Pete Fleming, and Nate Saint were massacred by the Huaorani tribe in Ecuador, many other missionaries, including Jim Elliot's widow, Elisabeth, rose up to take their places and minister to the Huaorani.

Untold thousands were inspired to missionary service by their example. Eventually, the Huaorani themselves became followers of Jesus. I once met the man who killed Nate Saint. He preached alongside his "son," Steve Saint. Steve isn't his real son, of course, but the son of the man he killed. Now, their shared faith in Jesus Christ unites them into one family. The two standing there together was a miracle of God's grace.

This has always been true—from the birth of the church until this very moment—that when Christians are put to death for their faith, they inspire multitudes more to take their places. As the apostle Paul put it, "For to me, to live is Christ and to die is gain" (Philippians 1:21).

So here we end our journey together.

I'll reiterate Father Tom's poignant words to those Yemeni nuns—those modern martyrs: "Let us be ready for martyrdom."

For the heart of our faith and his faith is the same. It's the same Jesus, it's the same mission, and it's the same Bible. It's the same love and the same passion. The only thing that might be different for us is our commitment to safety and security.

Probably no one wants to kill you today for your faith, but should your faith be any different from Father Tom's? Should my faith be any different?

We've explored the Martyr's Oath throughout this book, based upon that first Martyr's Oath I heard thousands pledge in India so long ago. Read that oath again and read it carefully, and let every line rest heavily on your heart.

It will tell you something. It will tell you whether Jesus is your security blanket or whether he's your life. It will show you the degree to which you're in love with this world or in love with Jesus.

These aren't easy questions, but this is not an easy world.

I'll leave you with the words of Brother Andrew, the founder of Open Doors and the author of *God's Smuggler*. Brother Andrew spent his entire life personally smuggling Bibles into the most dangerous parts of the world. I spent some time with him in his home not long ago. He often said these parting words to his dear friends who were prone to use a phrase many of us use almost every day: "Take care."

Brother Andrew would reply, "Never say *take care*. We don't *take care*. We *take risks*."

May you and I be fearless followers of Christ who, like Brother Andrew, take risks in fulfilling the mission of our selfless Lord.

# FOR ME TO LIVE IS CHRIST; FOR ME TO DIE IS GAIN

*I fully expect and hope that I will never be ashamed, but that I will continue to be bold for Christ, as I have been in the past. And I trust that my life will bring honor to Christ, whether I live or die.*

PHILIPPIANS 1:20, NLT

**RECENTLY THERE WAS A QUESTION** on the website Quora about the percentage of soldiers who serve in combat positions.[1] The answers varied. Some calculated that there were twelve soldiers behind the lines supporting every soldier who was on the front lines. Some said the answer was seven to one, others three to one. But one ex-soldier said this: *100 percent.*

I think they're all right in a way.

The stories I've shared in this book are from those who are on the front lines of the threats Christians are facing around the world. They are in combat: bullets are flying, shells are bursting, barrel bombs are exploding, and poison gas is wafting. And while it's easy to get discouraged when we see persecution around the world, especially as this persecution escalates, the outlook is far from hopeless. As I hope you saw in the stories and commentary throughout this book, these faithful brothers and sisters are leading the way to victory, as martyrs have done all through Christian history:

> They have defeated him [the devil] by the blood of the Lamb
>     and by their testimony.
> And they did not love their lives so much
>     that they were afraid to die.

REVELATION 12:11, NLT

But while these faithful ones are on the front lines, 100 percent of believers are in the army, and 100 percent of us can join the battle—and *must* join the battle. And that's what the Martyr's Oath is all about. While it may not be possible for all of us to join our brothers and sisters in the line of fire, it is possible for all of us to live for the Jesus they're willing to die for. I hope that as you've read their stories and learned about the realities they're facing, you've been inspired to examine your own faith and to say with the apostle Paul, "For to me, to live is Christ and to die is gain" (Philippians 1:21). As we live, we serve Jesus, wherever and however he calls us. And if in serving Jesus we die, we know that death has lost its sting (see 1 Corinthians 15:55, NLT); we know that to be "away from these earthly bodies" is to be "at home with the Lord" (2 Corinthians 5:8, NLT).

If you're ready to stand with Christians around the world and take the Martyr's Oath, I encourage you to visit www.MartyrsOath .com and take your stand. Then I encourage you to explore ways that you can more effectively support those on the front lines. Here are some ideas.

## PRAY FOR THEM—AND FAST

You already know to pray for those who are being persecuted and likely are already doing that. But here are some specific things you can pray for. Pray . . .

- that they remain strong in faith;
- that they remain fearless in witness;
- that they remain winsome and abound in love and forgiveness;
- that they sense the nearness of God and the comfort of the Holy Spirit;
- that they bring to mind the words of Scripture, along with psalms, hymns, and spiritual songs;
- that God would protect them from physical and psychological abuse and bring swift healing from those effects;
- that they exercise the gifts of the Spirit and display the fruit of the Spirit;
- that their persecutors will come to faith in Christ; and
- that their churches will grow and be undetected by the authorities.

## GET INVOLVED

Prayer is the most important step, and it's also something we all can do, regardless of circumstances, talents, or time. But here are a few other ways you can help our persecuted brothers and sisters:

- Let your political leaders know your concerns about oppressed Christians in Asia, the Middle East, the Horn of Africa, and North Africa.

- Demonstrate the love of Christ and the fruit of the Spirit to those around you—and especially to refugees. Don't shun Muslims in your community; be winsome. The fields are "white unto harvest," and as I've written in chapter 12, this is a unique time of opportunity for the church.
- Use the unique gifts God has given you for the benefit of those who are persecuted. In whatever vocation you find yourself, in whatever position of influence, in whatever circumstances, with whatever finances, in whatever health, God has blessed you with unique talents and opportunities, and part of praying for God's "kingdom come, [his] will be done in earth, as it is in heaven" (Matthew 6:10, KJV) is being willing to be used according to God's purposes. Pray that God would show you a unique way to support those who are being persecuted for their faith.

## GIVE

I cannot emphasize enough how important it is for us to provide financial support to the persecuted church. I don't care which organization you give to, but I beg you to give to a reputable one that ensures that our persecuted brothers and sisters are supported. You might also give to us, and we'll take care of helping the best organizations reach the most needy people. We will also continue to advocate around the world for international religious freedom and to stand against the persecution of Christians. Visit www.TheKAIROSTrust.com to learn more about us and our mission.

Regardless of the way that God calls you to follow him—whether you risk your life on the front lines or actively support those who are being persecuted through prayer and other action—I pray that you will know the extraordinary joy that comes only through serving Jesus. May we truly live for the Jesus that our brothers and sisters are willing to die for.

# ACKNOWLEDGMENTS

**WITH GRATITUDE TO MY AMAZING TEAM,** whose countless hours of work brought together all that you have read. I've never met more brilliant and committed people:

- Daniel Lidwin
- Melody Matzdorff
- Rick Nash
- Joann Webster
- Jonathan Williams

Then there are the countless sources whom I cannot name for their personal safety. This breaks my heart because I could not have done this without you. But you know who you are.

# APPENDIX 1

# THE MARTYR'S OATH

Consider taking your stand with Christians around the world in harm's way at www.MartyrsOath.com:

**I AM A FOLLOWER OF JESUS.** I believe he lived and walked among us, was crucified for our sins, and was raised from the dead, according to the Scriptures. I believe he is the King of the earth, who will come back for his church.

As he has given his life for me, so I am willing to give my life for him. I will use every breath I possess to boldly proclaim his gospel. Whether in abundance or need, in safety or peril, in peace or distress, I will not—I cannot—keep quiet. His unfailing love is better than life, and his grace compels me to speak his name even if his name costs me everything. Even in the face of death, I will not deny him. And should shadow and darkness encroach upon me, I will not fear, for I know he is always with me.

Though persecution may come, I know my battle is not against flesh but against the forces of evil. I will not hate those whom God has called me to love. Therefore, I will forgive when ridiculed, show mercy when struck, and love when hated. I will clothe myself with meekness and kindness so those around me may see the face of Jesus reflected in me, especially if they abuse me.

I have taken up my cross; I have laid everything else down. I know my faith could cost me my life, but I will follow and love Jesus until the end, whenever and however that end may come. Should I die for Jesus, I confess that my death is not to achieve salvation but in gratitude for the grace I've already received. I will not die to earn my reward in heaven, but because Jesus has already given me the ultimate reward in the forgiveness of my sins and the salvation of my soul.

For me to live is Christ; for me to die is gain.

*In Jesus' name,*
*Amen.*

# APPENDIX 2
# METHODOLOGY

**ALL THE PEOPLE** in the stories of this book are real, and their stories are true. We conducted interviews in person around the world in dozens of locations. Local leaders provided the contacts, and we conducted outside corroboration of the details provided by these persecuted Christians.

We tell their stories using their exact words, making minor adjustments only for clarity and grammar. We then meticulously changed the names, many personal descriptions, some details, and in some cases the locations, in order to obscure their identities and protect them.

Otherwise our work might have risked the lives of those we aim to save and whose lives are bringing new life to countless others.

# NOTES

**INTRODUCTION**

1. The ministry continues today under the leadership of his amazing son, Samuel Thomas. See *Hopegivers*, www.hopegivers.org.
2. Michael F. Haverluck, "Every 5 Minutes, a Christian Is Martyred," *One News Now*, September 20, 2015, http://www.onenewsnow.com/persecution /2015/09/20/every-5-minutes-a-christian-is-martyred.

**CHAPTER 1: I Am a Follower of Jesus**

1. George Weigel, "Rediscovering the Martyrology," *First Things*, February 26, 2014, https://www.firstthings.com/web-exclusives/2014/02 /rediscovering-the-martyrology.
2. Stephen Rand, "Freedom of Religion and the Persecution of Christians: The Open Doors Report, 2016," Open Doors, https://www.opendoorsuk.org /persecution/documents/ww-report-160113.pdf.
3. Bill Chappell, "World's Muslim Population Will Surpass Christians This Century, Pew Says," *The Two-Way*, April 2, 2015, http://www.npr.org /sections/thetwo-way/2015/04/02/397042004/muslim-population-will -surpass-christians-this-century-pew-says.
4. Bring Back Our Girls' Facebook page, accessed March 22, 2017, https:// www.facebook.com/bringbackourgirls/.
5. Report drawn from live interview; Aminu Abubakar, "As Many as 200 Girls Abducted by Boko Haram, Nigerian Officials Say," CNN, April 16, 2014, http:// www.cnn.com/2014/04/15/world/africa/nigeria-girls-abducted/; Aminu Abubakar, Faith Karimi, and Michael Pearson, "Scared but Alive: Video Purports to Show Abducted Nigerian Girls," CNN, May 13, 2014, http://www .cnn.com/2014/05/12/world/africa/nigeria-abducted-girls/; and David Blair, "Boko Haram Releases New Video Claiming to Show Nigeria's Abducted Chibok Schoolgirls," *Telegraph*, August 14, 2016, http://www.telegraph.co.uk/news /2016/08/14/boko-haram-releases-new-video-of-alleged-chibok-girls/.
6. There are many great organizations you can give to in order to help them. You can contribute to World Help (www.worldhelp.net), Open Doors

(www.opendoorsusa.org), or our own emergency relief fund, The KAIROS Trust (www.TheKAIROSTrust.com).

## CHAPTER 2: I Am Willing to Give My Life

1. Yaroslav Trofimov, "Behind Boko Haram's Split: A Leader Too Radical for Islamic State," *Wall Street Journal*, September 15, 2016, https://www.wsj.com/articles/behind-boko-haram-s-split-a-leader-too-radical-for-islamic-state-1473931827.
2. Michael Gryboski, "Expert: More Christians Killed Last Year in Northern Nigeria Than Rest of World Combined," *Christian Post*, November 15, 2013, http://www.christianpost.com/news/expert-more-christians-killed-last-year-in-northern-nigeria-than-rest-of-world-combined-108796/.
3. Dietrich Bonhoeffer, *The Cost of Discipleship* (New York: Touchstone, 1995), 89.

## CHAPTER 3: I Will Boldly Proclaim His Gospel

1. For a description of the helicopter method, see page 74.
2. Rev. Thomas Adams, *An Exposition upon the Second Epistle General of St. Peter*, chapter 1, verse 16, Google Books e-book.

## CHAPTER 4: Whether in Abundance or Need, in Safety or Peril, in Peace or Distress, I Will Not Keep Quiet

1. Jon D. Wilke, "Churchgoers Believe in Sharing Faith, Most Never Do," LifeWay, accessed March 24, 2017, http://www.lifeway.com/Article/research-survey-sharing-christ-2012.
2. Watchman Nee was a twentieth-century author, church planter, and Christian teacher in China. Nee was imprisoned for his faith after the Communist revolution.

## CHAPTER 5: His Unfailing Love Is Better than Life

1. Tim Lister et al., "ISIS Goes Global: 143 Attacks in 29 Countries Have Killed 2,043," CNN, February 13, 2017, http://www.cnn.com/2015/12/17/world/mapping-isis-attacks-around-the-world/.
2. Kevin Johnson, "Anxiety Grows over ISIL Recruits in U.S.," *USA Today*, November 14, 2015, https://www.usatoday.com/story/news/2015/11/14/isil-recruits-in-us-worry-officials/75774094/.

## CHAPTER 6: His Grace Compels Me to Speak His Name Even If His Name Costs Me Everything

1. "Palestinians Used Bible as Toilet Paper," *World Net Daily*, May 18, 2005, http://www.wnd.com/2005/05/30366/.
2. C. S. Lewis, *Mere Christianity* (New York: HarperOne, 1980), 86.

## CHAPTER 7: Even in the Face of Death, I Will Not Deny Him

1. Robert P. George and Thomas J. Reese, "Is Eritrea the North Korea of Africa?" *Christian Science Monitor*, August 18, 2015, http://

www.csmonitor.com/World/Africa/Africa-Monitor/2015/0818/Is-Eritrea-the
-North-Korea-of-Africa.

2. Yishai Halper, "'The North Korea of Africa': Where You Need a Permit to Have
Dinner with Friends," *Haaretz*, September 7, 2012, http://www.haaretz.com
/israel-news/the-north-korea-of-africa-where-you-need-a-permit-to-have
-dinner-with-friends-1.463319.

3. United States Department of State, *Eritrea 2014 International Religious
Freedom Report*, Bureau of Democracy, Human Rights, and Labor,
accessed March 29, 2017, http://www.state.gov/documents
/organization/238424.pdf.

4. George and Reese, "Is Eritrea the North Korea of Africa?" http://www
.csmonitor.com/World/Africa/Africa-Monitor/2015/0818/Is-Eritrea-the
-North-Korea-of-Africa.

5. Foreign & Commonwealth Office ,"Corporate Report: Eritrea—Country of
Concern," Gov.uk, January 21, 2015, https://www.gov.uk/government
/publications/eritrea-country-of-concern/eritrea-country-of-concern#torture.

6. Nik Ripken with Gregg Lewis, *The Insanity of God* (Nashville: B&H, 2013), 161.

**CHAPTER 8:** I Will Not Fear, for I Know He Is Always with Me

1. Isaac Abrak and Emma Ande, "Freed Nigerian Women Tell of Horror of Boko
Haram Captivity," Reuters, May 3, 2015, http://www.reuters.com
/article/us-nigeria-boko-haram-idUSKBN0NN0Q420150503.

**CHAPTER 9:** My Battle Is Not against Flesh

1. "Clarifying Some Misconceptions about the 'Three-Self,'" China Aid,
November 15, 2011, http://www.chinaaid.org/2011/11/clarifying-some
-misconceptions-about.html.

2. Eleanor Albert, "Religion in China," Council on Foreign Relations, June 10,
2015, http://www.cfr.org/china/religion-china/p16272.

3. Ian Johnson, "Church-State Clash in China Coalesces around a Toppled
Spire," *New York Times*, May 29, 2014, http://www.nytimes.com/2014/05
/30/world/asia/church-state-clash-in-china-coalesces-around-a-toppled
-spire.html

4. Coach Bill McCartney, *Promise Keepers Live 93*, released May 10, 1993,
Maranatha! Music, compact disc, track 17.

5. "Christian Persecution," Open Doors, accessed March 31, 2017, https://
www.opendoorsusa.org/christian-persecution/.

6. Brian J. Grim et al., "Religious Hostilities Reach Six-Year High," Pew Research
Center, January 14, 2014, http://www.pewforum.org/2014/01/14/religious
-hostilities-reach-six-year-high/.

**CHAPTER 12:** May Those around Me See the Face of Jesus Reflected in Me

1. "Dreams, Visions Moving Muslims to Christ," *CBN News*, April 8, 2015,
http://www1.cbn.com/cbnnews/insideisrael/2012/June/Dreams-Visions
-Moving-Muslims-to-Christ.

2. Lucinda Borkett-Jones, "'We Are Living in the Midst of the Greatest Turning of Muslims to Christ in History,'" *Christian Today*, June 17, 2015, http://www.christiantoday.com/article/we.are.living.in.the.midst.of.the.greatest.turning.of.muslims.to.christ.in.history/56393.htm.

3. Eliza Griswold, "Is This the End of Christianity in the Middle East?" *New York Times* magazine, July 22, 2015, http://www.nytimes.com/2015/07/26/magazine/is-this-the-end-of-christianity-in-the-middle-east.html

4. Borkett-Jones, "We Are Living in the Midst of the Greatest Turning of Muslims."

5. Mike Lanchin, "SS St. Louis: The Ship of Jewish Refugees Nobody Wanted," *BBC News*, May 13, 2014, http://www.bbc.com/news/magazine-27373131.

6. Beenish Ahmed, "America Turned Away Jewish Refugees Because Some Were Feared to Be Nazi Agents," *ThinkProgress*, November 19, 2015, https://thinkprogress.org/america-turned-away-jewish-refugees-because-some-were-feared-to-be-nazi-agents-b3f3524b182d#.hc310x8wt.

7. You can learn more about and support that work at www.TheKAIROS Trust.com.

## CHAPTER 13: I Have Taken Up My Cross

1. Vladimir Ilyich Lenin, "The Attitude of the Workers' Party to Religion," trans. Andrew Rothstein and Bernard Issacs, *Marxists Internet Archive*, accessed March 9, 2017, https://www.marxists.org/archive/lenin/works/1909/may/13.htm.

2. *The Black Book of Communism* apportions the body count this way: 65 million in the People's Republic of China, 20 million in the former Soviet Union, 2 million in Cambodia, 2 million in North Korea, 1.7 million in Africa, 1.5 million in Afghanistan, 1 million in the Eastern Bloc, 1 million in Vietnam, 150,000 in Latin America, and 10,000 deaths resulting from "the international Communist movement and Communist parties not in power." Jean-Louis Panné et al., *The Black Book of Communism* (Cambridge, MA: Harvard University Press, 1999), 4.

3. *Conservapedia*, s.v. "Atheism and Communism," last modified February 26, 2017, http://www.conservapedia.com/Atheism_and_Communism.

4. Ian Johnson, "Decapitated Churches in China's Christian Heartland," *New York Times*, May 21, 2016, http://www.nytimes.com/2016/05/22/world/asia/china-christians-zhejiang.html.

## CHAPTER 15: I Will Follow and Love Jesus until the End

1. I've abridged the account I received in the e-mail and made some small editorial changes for clarity.

## CONCLUSION For Me to Live Is Christ; For Me to Die Is Gain

1. "What Percentage of Soldiers Serve in Combat Positions?" Quora, accessed April 4, 2017, https://www.quora.com/What-percentage-of-Soldiers-serve-in-combat-positions.

# DISCUSSION GUIDE

## INTRODUCTION

1. The author went on a journey of transformation by seeing Jesus through the eyes of the persecuted church. Take an honest look at your heart. How would you describe your level of willingness to be transformed? What are your hesitations in entering this journey?

2. The author says, "The gospel has cost most of us nothing" (page xii). What is your reaction to that statement? Do you agree? Explain.

## CHAPTER 1: I AM A FOLLOWER OF JESUS

1. The author quotes 1 Corinthians 1:18: "The message of the cross is foolishness to those who are perishing" (page 2). Who in your life considers Christianity foolishness? Why do you think he or she perceives it this way?

2. The author writes, "I wonder how many of us in the United States have counted the cost of following Jesus—I mean *really* counted the cost. For some of us, we may think we have. We just don't think we need Jesus very much. Jesus is the ultimate 'value add' to whatever version of the good

life we've fashioned, the capstone to a life well lived"
(page 11). Would you say this is true in your life? What
things in your life, if you look deeply and honestly, might
you consider more important than following Jesus?

## CHAPTER 2: I AM WILLING TO GIVE MY LIFE

1. Rose survived severe cuts to her neck and arm, witnessed
   the horror of her husband and children being beheaded,
   lost the baby she was carrying, had her possessions stolen,
   temporarily lost custody of her daughter, escaped another
   attack from Boko Haram, and was robbed in her new shop.
   Rose's story is heartbreaking yet courageous. A striking
   statement her father said after all this is "Don't worry; life
   is more than possessions" (page 17). How do you think
   Rose responded? After reading Rose's story and consider-
   ing your own life, how do *you* respond?

2. The author asks, "Could it be that we are simply using Jesus
   as a means to assuage our consciences as we live for ourselves? We self-medicate on religion so we don't feel quite
   so bad about our total self-centeredness, our unabashed
   obsession with ourselves, our things, our future, and our
   lives" (page 19). How might this be true for you? More specifically, what "obsessions" do you have that might indi-
   cate you are living for yourself?

3. The author concludes the chapter by saying, "Rose was willing to give everything for Jesus because he gave everything
   for her. He also gave everything for *us*. The question is, are
   we willing to do the same for him?" (page 20). What would it
   look like for you to "give everything for Jesus"?

## CHAPTER 3: I WILL BOLDLY PROCLAIM HIS GOSPEL

1. The author states, "We live a life of love, and because of the transformation God has performed in us, we naturally tell others about him. If we aren't inclined to do so, then we aren't really experiencing the power of God in our lives" (pages 21–22). Why might you not be inclined to tell others about God and the transformation he has performed in you? What is holding you back?

2. The author poses convicting questions: "How can we take Jesus' peace for ourselves and so easily keep that peace from others by our silence and indifference? How could we stand with a life preserver in our arms while others drown in front of us?" (page 32). Whom does God want you to proclaim him to? Name two or three ways you can do it this week.

3. The author concludes this chapter by stating, "When we truly believe that Jesus gave his life for us, we, like Andrew, will be compelled to proclaim him wherever we are and wherever we go. And when we don't, we'll feel our consciences crying out to us. I'm concerned that too often we don't even know how to hear that quiet voice anymore" (pages 32–33). Do you know how to hear God's voice? What can you start doing to be able to hear his voice more clearly?

## CHAPTER 4: WHETHER IN ABUNDANCE OR NEED, IN SAFETY OR PERIL, IN PEACE OR DISTRESS, I WILL NOT KEEP QUIET

1. The author says, "[Those imprisoned for Jesus] get thrown into prisons; we build our own, walling ourselves in with our material possessions and boxing up our hearts with our greed. Eventually we can barely feel our faith

206 II THE MARTYR'S OATH

anymore" (page 44). The author suggests that empathy is one way to identify with our persecuted brothers and sisters, and empathy leads to action. The author challenges, "We should be asking ourselves, *As a light of the world, what light am I to shine in this?*" (page 46). What specific way might you today empathize and take action to help your persecuted brothers and sisters?

2.  The author states, "Many times throughout Scripture, God placed people in positions of wealth or influence in order to bring about his purposes, and surely he does so now. But abundance can also be a distraction and an excuse. We will never serve and love as we must until we find contentment in abundance or need, in safety or peril, in peace or distress" (page 46). Think of examples from your own life. When have you used wealth or influence "to bring about his purposes"? When has abundance served as "a distraction and an excuse" for you? How can you more consistently leverage your wealth and influence for others' benefit?

## CHAPTER 5: HIS UNFAILING LOVE IS BETTER THAN LIFE

1.  The author asks these important questions: "How deeply moved are you by the love of Jesus? Does it touch you, or have you become too accustomed to it, too used to his story?" (page 53). How would you answer?

2.  The author writes, "While it is natural and in many ways understandable to avoid danger, God provides the greatest blessings when we risk it all on love, when we run into desperate situations and witness the love of God to others" (page 54). Have you ever experienced this, or do you know

of someone close to you who has experienced this? What was the result?

3. First we experience the love of God and then we take baby steps to love others, the author explains on page 55. What are some baby steps you can take this week to love others more fully?

## CHAPTER 6: HIS GRACE COMPELS ME TO SPEAK HIS NAME EVEN IF HIS NAME COSTS ME EVERYTHING

1. The author describes the missionary Ermias: "He's so close to Jesus—and his belief in the gospel is so strong— that he's pulled like gravity to the next opportunity to tell someone else about Jesus" (page 67). When in your life have you felt so close to Jesus that you were pulled like gravity to tell someone about him? Whom did you tell, and what happened?

2. The author challenges us: "Jesus' grace compels us to share his love, especially when and where it's the hardest to share. It cuts through our desire to live cozy lives. . . . We need to make ourselves uncomfortable. We must sacrifice a little more than we're comfortable with, risk a little more than we're comfortable with, go to places we're uncomfortable to be in" (page 69). What would it look like for you to cut through your desire to live a cozy life or to do uncomfortable things in faith?

## CHAPTER 7: EVEN IN THE FACE OF DEATH, I WILL NOT DENY HIM

1. The author says, "For those of us living in safety, it seems we are willing to suffer so little to speak the name of Jesus"

(page 73). Why do you think safety limits our willingness to suffer "to speak the name of Jesus"?

2.  The author states, "We will never experience full Christian discipleship if we aren't persecuted or if we aren't praying for, praying with, or living alongside those who are persecuted" (page 88). Whom can you pray for or with this week that is experiencing persecution? What is his or her story? If no one comes to mind, begin praying for an opportunity and visit www.opendoorsusa.org.

## CHAPTER 8: I WILL NOT FEAR, FOR I KNOW HE IS ALWAYS WITH ME

1.  "When we believe in God, we are courageous. Courage is supernatural, and it draws from the confidence we have in God because of the love God has for us," the author explains on page 99. How is courage related to the love of God?

2.  The author challenges us: "The persecuted church proves to us that faith is stronger than fear. If they do not give in to fear when their faith faces such trials, then how is it that our fears bind us up so hopelessly?" (page 100). What fears bind you up when it comes to sharing your faith? How can faith overcome those fears?

## CHAPTER 9: MY BATTLE IS NOT AGAINST FLESH

1.  The author states, "The enemy would like nothing better than for us to keep our focus on our physical circumstances or on our enemies" (page 110). What distracts your focus from the spiritual battle we face as Christians? How can you keep your focus trained on the spiritual battle and not on your "physical circumstances or enemies"?

2. The author reminds us, "We recognize that just as those who persecute Christians now are blinded, we too were once enemies of Christ and were blind to our sin" (page 111). Think about your life before you followed Christ. How would you describe to someone that you were an enemy of Christ and blind to your sin?

3. "Never underestimate the power of prayer and the Word of God," the author challenges us (page 111). How much do you believe that? Have you witnessed the power of prayer or the Word of God change a situation? Explain.

## CHAPTER 10: I WILL FORGIVE

1. The author shares the stories of Sandy and Daniel. What circumstances did they face that might have kept them from forgiving those who wronged them? Why did they forgive anyway? What did forgiveness look like for them?

2. The author asks, "Christians around the world go through countless forms of suffering, yet God calls them to forgive their enemies. And they do it! What are our excuses for refusing to forgive ours?" (page 121). How would you answer this for yourself?

## CHAPTER 11: I WILL CLOTHE MYSELF WITH MEEKNESS

1. The author states, "Resistance to the gospel melts away as we demonstrate love to our persecutors, pray for them, and return blessing for cursing" (page 124). When in your life or in someone else's has this happened? What is the story? How have you seen this principle at work in the stories in this book?

2. Mebrahtu, the faithful Christian who shares his story, says, "Now I am ready to worship God and to lead others to him. It is my desire and my joy" (page 133). Do you share his sentiment? How would you describe what you are ready to do? What is your desire and your joy? If it differs from Mebrahtu's, why?

3. The author asks, "It can be difficult for us, in a society that worships strength and fame and celebrity, to clothe ourselves in meekness, but that is what we are called to do. If meekness is 'strength under control,' how can we exhibit that in our culture the way our persecuted brothers and sisters are doing in theirs?" (page 134). How would you answer that question? What would it look like for you to exhibit "strength under control"?

## CHAPTER 12: MAY THOSE AROUND ME SEE THE FACE OF JESUS REFLECTED IN ME

1. The author says, "The Martyr's Oath statement that frames this chapter is 'May those around me see the face of Jesus reflected in me,' but too often our version is something like 'May those around me see the face of Jesus reflected in me as long as it doesn't make me uncomfortable or unpopular or unsafe or poor or less powerful or less important'" (page 151). Which of these fears most causes you to hesitate reflecting Jesus to others: being uncomfortable, unpopular, unsafe, poor, less powerful, or less important? Why does this fear have power over you?

2. The author ends the chapter by stating, "We must be prepared to share Jesus with others—regardless of the cost—whether around the world or in our own backyards"

(page 154). For some or many of us, traveling to other places in the world may not be an option right now. But we have people in our own backyards—our neighborhoods, our schools, our places of work, even in our families—who don't know Jesus. Whom is God wanting you to reach out to, and how can you be prepared to share Jesus with that person?

## CHAPTER 13: I HAVE TAKEN UP MY CROSS

1. The author explains, "'Taking up our cross' means conditioning ourselves to understand that sacrifice is a regular experience. Sacrifice is the front line of a war we have with ourselves and our sinful nature. Sacrifice is the beginning of service and the cost of becoming a witness to the world!" (page 166). What sacrifices are you willing to make for Jesus? What lifestyle changes can you make to condition yourself to regularly sacrifice?

2. The author gives us this humbling challenge: "We should be prepared to die because the central symbol of our faith reminds us of Jesus' death and of his call to 'follow me'" (page 166). What would it look like for you to be willing to accept this challenge—to follow Jesus even to death? What steps can you take to make yourself more willing?

## CHAPTER 14: I HAVE LAID EVERYTHING ELSE DOWN

1. The author states, "For American Christians, where our default trajectory is comfort and safety, sometimes it is necessary for us to *choose* discomfort and sacrifice and even suffering in order to identify with Christ and with our

brothers and sisters who are suffering in the world" (page 177). What does it look like to "choose discomfort and sacrifice"? What do we learn by choosing discomfort and sacrifice?

2.   "When we consider whether we've already laid everything down or are ready to, let me suggest to you that a good first step might be to unplug from everything else," the author advises on pages 178–79. What do you need to unplug from in order to lay everything down? Name at least one goal you can set in order to condition yourself to lay down your life.

## CHAPTER 15: I WILL FOLLOW AND LOVE JESUS UNTIL THE END

1.   The author challenges us to read the Martyr's Oath again and let it sink into our hearts. He says, "It will show you the degree to which you're in love with this world or in love with Jesus" (page 186). In what ways are you in love with this world? In what ways are you in love with Jesus?

2.   The author ends the chapter with this: "May you and I be fearless followers of Christ who . . . take risks in fulfilling the mission of our selfless Lord" (page 186). What risks might God be calling you to take today?

## CONCLUSION: FOR ME TO LIVE IS CHRIST; FOR ME TO DIE IS GAIN

1.   Which persecuted brothers and sisters can you be praying for consistently?

2.   What way or ways can you get involved in practically helping persecuted believers?

3. The author ends by saying, "I pray that you will know the extraordinary joy that comes only through serving Jesus" (page 191). Recall the stories that were shared in this book. Describe the joy present in the believers' stories. What circumstances were they facing? What was the source of their joy? How have you experienced joy in serving Jesus?

# ABOUT THE AUTHOR

**JOHNNIE MOORE,** author of the highly acclaimed *Defying ISIS*, is a speaker and a humanitarian who has been called one of the "world's most influential young leaders" and "a modern-day Dietrich Bonhoeffer." His advocacy has provided tens of millions of dollars in emergency assistance to persecuted Christians, and in 2015 he helped lead the charge to get genocide resolutions against ISIS passed unanimously in both houses of the United States Congress and in the British and European parliaments. He is a member of the White House Faith Advisory Council and is a recipient of the prestigious medal of valor from the Simon Wiesenthal Center. Moore is also a widely read opinion columnist, having written for the *Washington Post*, Fox News, *Relevant* magazine, and CNN. He is a visiting lecturer at the Liberty University Center for Apologetics and Cultural Engagement, a fellow of the Townsend Institute for Leadership and Counseling at Concordia University, and an international spokesperson for the Museum of the Bible. He serves on the boards of the National Association of Evangelicals, the World Evangelical Alliance, World Help, the Dream Center LA, the Anti-Defamation League of Los Angeles, and My Faith Votes. He is the founder of The KAIROS Company.

**Some estimate that every five minutes a Christian is martyred for his or her faith.**

*What in the world is going on?*

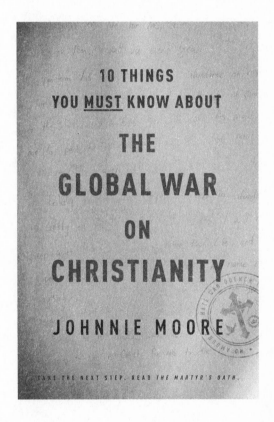

This ancillary booklet to *The Martyr's Oath* will help readers discover how pervasive and brutal the persecution of Christians is in today's world.

**www.tyndale.com**

The KAIROS
Trust provides
financial support
to and advocacy
for Christians
globally, especially
those who face
persecution for
their faith.